WE THE DECEIVED

The Power of Systemic Norms

Josh Chamberlain

INTRODUCTION

So who am I? I am a retired person who had a career involving incident management and tactical knowledge, I was also in a management position. So what is this? This is a look at all things assumption based in our civilizations political and legal systems. In other words we will be examining paradigms or fundamental assumptions that make us assume 'that's just the way it is'.

I am also a person who has followed and studied politics for nearly thirty years. I have made a concerted effort to know what is going on in The United States and the world for that matter.

So let's dive into some history to lay a foundation to question what is and what is just accepted as 'the way it is'. After laying the foundation we can look at the present day and it's paradigms. As you can see in the table of contents, I am attempting to cover many issues from the perspectives of existing paradigms.

TABLE OF CONTENTS

CHAPTER 1 EARLY SYSTEMS

'Just the way it was'

I have enough faith in your intelligence to know you understand the basics. For example, in ancient history and not so ancient history we had kings, queens, conquerors, empires, tyrants and tribes of every sort. Including Native American to tribes in the Amazon Basin. For thousands of years we had one brutal guy at the top, we had his or her tyrannical rule and if people wanted to live they should just fall in line.

My goal in this chapter is to illustrate how systems were developed in ancient times. Most importantly we see that people understood these systems as fundamental assumptions or paradigms that were accepted by all. So what's the point? The point is simple, these examples illustrate that the existing system of governments and laws have vast influence on the people. 'The people' will do what they are forced to do and they will accept the system they are under as a fundamental paradigm. Here is a clip from wikipedia on Draconian law in ancient Greece dating back to the year 620 BC.

Athens

One of the earliest datable events in Athenian history is the creation of the Draconian Law code. 620 BC. We know little about Draco and the code, with the homicide law being the only one known due to it surviving the Solonian reforms. The law seems to have distinguished between premeditated and involuntary homicide, and provided for the reconciliation of the killer with the family of the dead man. The homicide law of Draco was still in force in the fourth century Though the rest of the code is unknown, it was by Athenian tradition known to have been very harsh.

To this day you will still hear people in the media and academic circles coining the term "Draconian" as a descriptive way to point out brutal acts of every kind. In the wikipedia quote above it mentions "reconciliation of the killer with the family of the dead man". Translation, if your family member was killed and the murderer and was caught you and your family had the right to kill the murderer yourselves up close and personal. This was probably viewed as a common sense way to administer justice. You killed my family member now we will kill you, case closed. To imagine this now it seems primitive but to the people of these times in Greece it was just the normal order of business. The system is the system and the people do not generally question it. They simply just fall in line and go with it.

On a side note I wonder why, of all of the terms available, why do people like to use the term draconian in the present day?

After all, this word is over 2600 years old and named after some guy Draco. I personally think they like the word because it sounds ominous and kind of sounds like Dracula. So now when you hear this word used on the news you will know the origins and be able to judge if the thing, event or policy is in fact draconian in nature.

As I mentioned in the introduction I worked in a tactical management position for 20 years. I've seen the best and the worst in human nature nature in just about every kind of incident. I know that some of you will look at Draconian law with regards to murder and justice and say "hey, sounds good to me!" If I were to choose to embrace the darker side of my own human nature I would certainly agree. But I think the point of talking about advanced civilization is to understand that what separates us from the animals is, to not embrace the so called 'darker angels of our nature'. I think we all know this (for the most part).

Now that we have Greece examined, let's take a look at Rome. Here is an interesting snippet from wikipedia on the Senate of the (Roman Republic).

**The ethical requirements of senators were significant. Senators could not engage in banking or any form of public contract. They could not own a ship that was large enough to participate in foreign commerce, and they could not leave Italy without permission from the Senate. In addition, since they were not paid, individuals usually sought to become a senator only if they were independently wealthy.**

**While in session, the Senate had the power to act on its own, and even against the will of the presiding magistrate if it wished. The** *__presiding magistrate began each meeting with a speech which was usually brief, but was sometimes a lengthy oration. The presiding magistrate would then begin a discussion by referring an issue to the senators, who would discuss the issue, one at a time, by order of seniority, with the first to speak, the most senior senator, known as the Princep Sanatus (leader of the Senate), who was then followed by ex-consuls (consulares), and then the praetors and ex-praetors (praetorii). This continued, until the most junior senators had spoken. Senators who had held magisterial office always spoke before those who had not, and if a Patrician was of equal seniority as a Plebian the patrician would always speak first.__*

__A senator could make a brief statement, discuss the matter in detail, or talk about an unrelated topic. All senators had to speak before a vote could be held, and since all meetings had to end by nightfall, a senator could talk a proposal to death (a filibuster) if they could keep the debate going until nightfall. It is known, for example, that the senator Cato The Younger once filibustered in an attempt to prevent the Senate from granting Julius Caesar a law that would have given land to the veterans of Pompey.__

This voting and debating Senate was formed in the year 753 BC. Does any of this sound familiar? This was over 2700 years ago, you had a Senate leader, you had issues brought forth by this leader. Debate with one Senator at a time took place making opening statements and you had a vote in the end. They even had a filibuster as we do now in our own congress. This was the Roman's great experiment just like our country is known as the great experiment. At the time the Roman empire with it's Senate considered itself the pinnacle of modern civilization and this all took place thousands of years ago. But there were certain fundamental assumptions never questioned by these Senators because that's just the way it was.

CHAPTER 2

'Left Overs'

So we have a Senate in the United States and the Romans had a Senate with debates and votes and filibusters. Yet we have stark differences between the two Republics that are worthy of mention with regards to comparison. Firstly our Senators are elected by the people versus the Romans who placed Senators to the position based on the social status of the person. They were automatically placed in the Senate by law. In spite of these differences, I feel it necessary to acknowledge that many people believe that the United States is in a similar moral decline. We saw in Rome as it imploded from within after hundreds of years of ruling as an empire.

Empires are another difference worth mentioning. The United States in my opinion is not looking to conquer the world. I think we respect the sovereignty of nations even though in my opinion we exert a conquest of influence all over the world. We are in the habit of defeating an enemy like Nazi Germany and just giving the country back. Yet we must take notice that every country we have defeated have generally become Democracies. Iraq on the other hand I feel is some kind of Democratic Islamic State hybrid. It reminds me of Obama Care. It's a hybrid of company paid insurance and Socialized Medicine. I don't think that either hybrid has been a truly effective solution. Your either a

Democracy or an Islamic Republic. You either have socialized government provided medicine or you have free market capitalism style employer provided medical insurance. You really just can't mix these things successfully in my opinion.

Now let us examine the leftover paradigms in the establishment of the Roman Senate. As I mentioned previously, the Roman Senate was the pinnacle of advanced civilization and the voice of reason in it's time. But what paradigms were left over in spite of this crucial invention of a Roman Senate? The Romans did establish a form of orderly government yet in my opinion the freedom of the citizens of Rome was never really a priority in my view. Rome engaged in global conquest, and we have all heard of the famed gladiator arena known as the coliseum. They used general terrorism everywhere they invaded using things like torture and crucifiction. Many other techniques were employed to keep the population in line wherever they invaded. The general message to the conquered people was simple. We will allow you to live in peace and you will pay taxes to Rome. If you rise up against us we will crucify a thousand people or worse every time you step out of line. So in spite of being the reasonable civilized light of the world the Romans sheer brutality were leftovers that existed as the paradigms of the age. Again the people and rulers said "that's just the way it is". This is again my personal view.

These examples of absolute rule and total terroristic control and brutality existed on a global level throughout the entirety of most of history. The Mongols, the Japanese, the British Empire and the list goes on and on. So why am I starting my book with a history lesson and a lot of talk about paradigms or fundamental assumptions? One of the main points I want to make about paradigms is that they are meant to be changed. They can be changed for good or evil and for a huge selection of reasons.

For example the Paradigm of the Shah in Iran (1), he was a person we liked very much as the leader of Iran. He was reasonable and the people of Iran were relatively free to live in peace and harmony. When the Islamic revolution (2) took place that paradigm of freedom changed and the Ayatollah took power and established a total and very strict Islamic State.

This new paradigm has been in place for decades and now the people of Iran can not even access the internet. Sharia Law is enforced and we all know they chant "Death to Israel" and "Death to America" in the streets. They have become an existential threat to both Israel and the United States. Everyone knows they are going to develop nuclear weapons in my opinion. Islam is a tricky issue to understand. On the one hand we have these really nice people in the United States who are nice to talk to and obey our laws. Yet in some places like Michigan (3) we have huge Islamic communities that wish to be separated into a so called (no go zone) for police and they want to practice the enforcement of Sharia Law right here. They can't just have a separate country of different laws than we have on the federal and state levels. Yet in some places in Europe they actually do have no go zones.

But when you examine Islamic Countries like Iran, Saudi Arabia and many others they are doing things that boggle the American mind as a matter of common law. Those are the nation states of Islam (4). I am not referring to terrorist organizations like ISIS (5) and all the rest. Islamic paradigms are a little different yet they are what I call a left over from ancient times. What people don't tend to know is that Islamist don't view the Koran the same way christians view the Bible. Christians view the Bible as a book that can be interpreted in many ways. Since the Schism of the Catholic Church carried out by Martin Luther (6), we have seen the development of thousands of Protestant Denominations. Before this, the Catholic or Universal Church was the authority on the entire Christian religion in the world.

With Islam we see the prophet Mohhamed who was, according to Islamist, (receiving and writing the literal words of God himself). So because these writings are the literal words of God they are not subject to interpretation with the exception of some verses considered implied and not literal (7). These writings are therefore timeless truths given by God that are to generally be taken literally forever. Many people wonder why Islamic countries live like it's 600 years ago. The reason is because Islam started 600 years ago. So these timeless eternal words of God are the same to Islamist yesterday today and forever. So we see things like stonings and throwing homosexuals off the tops of buildings. Then we see these beheadings in Saudi Arabia are just Islamist doing Gods will as instructed by the Koran. So on the one hand I can call this a brutal leftover from history, but it's not going to change any time soon. This is a God based paradigm in Islam. If one believes that beheadings and stonings are holy acts directed by God, they can do pretty much anything. So in essence they see certain brutalities as a literal holy act. Terrorist are extremist in there form of Islam but they still have the same thing in common. They believe terrorism is not terrorism, they believe it is a holy act. They believe God will reward what they do.

So in observing the present day in the United States, what is our current state in the governance of our country? Well for starters in 2018 only 53 percent of eligible voters turned out for the midterm election. This was the highest voter turnout in forty years (8). Most people in the present day believe that politicians are corrupt without a doubt. Most people believe that the government couldn't care less about them. People who follow politics realize that lobbyists create a situation in which everyone in congress are basically bought and paid for (9). Elections are dependant on raising money for candidates. Big business pays billions of dollars every year to buy politicians who will assist them in many ways to make money in my opinion.

The people are completely divided right down the middle, left or right they choose to take sides in this pageant that really feels like professional wrestling. When I look at the whole thing I just see one giant corrupt and confusing mess. And right now 'that's just the way it is', this mess is our new paradigm. In my opinion, many people just can't stand politics and simply ignore the whole thing. Many people can't stand even watching the news because it's just too miserable, argumentative and depressing. I can assure you that this mess is not what the founding fathers had in mind at all. So what on earth happened to our country? How did we get here? Why did we get here? What can be done at this point? And like every problem, there is usually some root cause or causes. So what are they? Let's see if we can untangle this whole jumbled up three ring circus.

CHAPTER 3

'The great experiment the United States'

According to history (as I recall), the war with England was started over taxation without representation. Then we had the Boston Tea Party. Well whatever the reason, a bunch of English rebels decided they wanted to be free from the King of England. That seems a bit too simple to me but that's what we are taught in grade school. England had decided to go into the New World and make it part of the British Empire. The new world was a great prize on so many levels. It probably came down to money and commerce and a host of other riches that could come from such a vast and fertile land. So we had Patriots (rebels) and we had Loyalist (non rebels). So in the beginning how did our dreams of independence from England and the idea that all people are free, apply to these English Loyalist? They were treated brutally and in some cases they were tarred and feathered (10). After the war was over they either had to fend for themselves or flee (10). So no loyalist party was ever formed which I guess is understandable given that's just the way it was back then. In today's political climate the loyalist would be given freedom of speech and welfare and could apply for political asylum at the nearest port of entry and go to a sanctuary city in my opinion.

So England is finally defeated in the New World and our founding fathers come up with an invention. A system of government unique in the history of the world (for the most part). The founding fathers were absolutely brilliant. A government by the people of the people and for the people. So how did they possibly come up with this idea? They in my opinion threw away every paradigm of every system of government. The people will be free and the people will elect representatives to speak there needs and wishes to the new Government. A system of checks and balances would be established to assure that the people never fell victim to a Kingship or Dictatorship. They decided on three branches of government operating in unity to establish checks and balances. The Senate (like Rome) and the House of Representatives would be the legislative branch or lawmakers. The Executive Branch or the President. And the Judicial Branch which equates to the court system up to the Supreme Court. All of these branches are designed to keep the others in check. Then they created the United States Constitution. This is the rule book that these branches have to follow as a matter of law (11). All of this combined is a new and revolutionary system of government that protects the people's freedom and basically makes them the voice of influence over the government.

In the beginning of our government politicians were not paid anything. They had full time jobs or had amassed wealth already. They were paid per diem to cover things like lodging and food. (12) but not a set salary. This was also the case in Rome to a degree. The Roman Senators were not compensated yet they were already rich. So Rome was a Republic and so are we. The difference is that we are a Democratic Republic (13). As we know from the Pledge of allegiance. "And to the Republic for which it stands". These early politicians were very smart men but more importantly they were men of character. So what difference does it make that they were men of moral decency and character? These men wanted to truly do the right thing for the people they represented. In other words they cared about the prosperity and well being of the people.

CHAPTER 4

'Moral Relativism'

What is moral relativism (14). It is simply the idea that morality is relative. In other words, morality is simply the opinion of each individual. It almost seems to make sense to many people. I think they see this as a right. I have the right to decide what's moral to me and you have the right to decide what's moral for you. It sounds like freedom. In the past this was not the case. Morality in the masses was completely black and white.

Everyone in the thirties and forties dressed differently they went out in suits quite often. They went to church on Sunday and wore their "Sunday Best". People have always had the propensity to do evil things and commit crimes throughout the entire history of the world. One must however take notice of the fact that back in the thirties and forties we did not have anything resembling the crime of today. Sure they had the mob but they did not have mass shootings in schools, heroin and fentanyl epidemics and fifty plus people shot in Chicago every weekend (15) and similar shootings in most large cities. No drug cartels, no 911 terrorist attacks, no ISIS and far fewer serial killers. The majority of people could keep the front door unlocked at night.

So common decency was a shared value by the majority of people. Make no mistake it wasn't a perfect utopia and plenty of bad things happened. But the difference between now and then is enormous. So how did moral relativism begin? At some point in the 1950's university professors introduced this notion of moral relativism to the students. These students with degrees ate this up in the 50's and especially in the 60's. So this is called progressive education. The irony of the term progressive is that it implies some form of progress. Was moral relativism a form of American progress? The crime stats certainly don't agree with that notion. Yet we did see quite substantial gun related shootings in the 30s and 40's. Much of it was Mob related and interpersonal crimes or vigilante crimes regarding relationship infidelity (16). In spite of this, many people do still do see right and wrong as a black and white issue. Moral relativism is not the main problem in my opinion. Think of the country as having an open wound. Moral relativism and progressive education are a sort of salt being poured into the larger wound in our modern culture.

CHAPTER 5

'Leftovers part 2'

As we discussed earlier the founding fathers established the three branches of government. The constitution created a system that would last forever in protecting the freedom of the people and providing for all the people's needs (11). These needs range from law and order to protection from our enemies. So for about thirty years, I have always felt that something was broken in the whole system. Some paradigm that nobody ever questions, something infecting the very fabric of the founding fathers intentions for us. The way the founding fathers viewed the leaders of our government was through the assumption that men of character would operate honestly. They would always have the best interest of the people in mind.

At that time they adopted a left over paradigm from the Roman Senate. The basic idea was that the Congress would debate issues in the creation of laws. So the plan was to let them fight the issues out via debate and come to a final conclusion and conduct a vote. This would also apply to the judicial branch. People charged with crimes needed to have due process and a fair trial by a jury of their peers. So when a trial is conducted or even a bench trial the accused has a right to representation. Everyone is afforded the right to a lawyer and the prosecution has a right to present the case of the State. When elections are held the candidates will have debates and debate why they are the best choice. This is a huge paradigm called the **adversarial system of government** (17). It kind of makes sense if everyone engaging in it is honest and seeking the truth. But this leftover paradigm adopted by us from the Roman Senate debates is actually a huge problem. Now I know what your thinking "this has always been this way" I never even thought about it. How can this be a problem? I will explain this paradigm and its effects on our great experiment and how it has mutated and permeated just about every part of our American culture.

CHAPTER 6

'Ocean of Kool Aid'

I make a concerted effort to not use cliches. The definition of a cliche is basically a common saying that lacks original thought. For example, "one man's trash is another man's treasure". But I'm making an exception here. I'm sure that most of you have heard the cliche "drinking the Kool Aid". This saying in my opinion has its roots in the infamous JonesTown massacre. I'll paste this from the internet for those who are not familiar with this horrific event.

**(On November 18, 1978, in what became known as the "Jonestown Massacre," more than 900 members of an American cult called the Peoples Temple died in a mass suicide-murder under the direction of their leader Jim Jones.) (18)**

These poor souls drank poisoned Kool Aid containing cyanide and other chemicals (18). Why did they do it? This Cult was gradually brainwashed by Jim Jones the cult leader. Like all cult leaders Jim Jones had a great deal of charisma and was an expert manipulator and an expert liar. So now we have this cliche saying "don't drink the Kool Aid". So what would be a simple example of drinking the so called Kool Aid? In the past buying a car was only done in one way. You went to the dealership and some man or woman came out to greet you. The sales person gathered basic information about what your price range was and what you were looking for. Once this information was conveyed the sales person started a sales technique by saying whatever they had to say to manipulate you into buying the car they wanted sell you. They would say anything they could to manipulate you and exercise deceptive lies into convincing you that this was a great deal and that you are really getting a good deal on the car.

All of this manipulation and lying was just part of the game. Yet the customer in most cases knew that this person was lying and manipulating them. So this game began to advance to the haggling phase of this game of lies and manipulation. If you made a counter offer several times you would eventually find out what the real best deal was. If you did this and got the best deal, congratulations, you did not 'drink the Kool Aid' of this lying self serving manipulating sales person. If you just agreed to the offer by sales person you "drank the Kool Aid". But in all fairness this person was just trying to make a living within the established car sales paradigm. This still happens now at dealerships but some car sales companies have abandoned this and we even see commercials about car vending machines (19). This is smart, because people don't generally appreciate being lied to and manipulated. I think that many people dread having to buy a car and have to deal with this game. So what is the point of this example? The point is that we are all either dishing out or drinking the Kool Aid or we are too smart to drink it.

The average person has accepted the fact that our government system and politicians are doing nothing less than lying to us and manipulating us. I will go through this in detail and you may be surprised how pervasive the manipulation and deception of the masses is in our time. As I sit here writing on my computer right now I have the news going on the TV. I can hear the live impeachment hearing of President Donald Trump in congress. I hear the Democrats Kool Aid which is to compliment the witnesses and make them out to be patriotic heroes exposing the corrupt and evil President. I also hear the Republican Kool Aid which is to destroy the validity and credibility of the witnesses in order to protect the President from being impeached. But what is their real purpose in these Public Hearings on both sides? The real purpose here is to compete with each other for the sole purpose of manipulating your views and they will all say anything to twist the truth in order to manipulate and influence the people of the United States.

So what is the paradigm here? The paradigm is, that it is perfectly acceptable within the adversarial system of government for politicians to say and do anything to influence and manipulate your opinion and beliefs. No amount of manipulation and twisting of the truth is off limits. So should we question this paradigm? I say yes and here is why. It was never the intention of our founding fathers to lie to and manipulate the people of the United States. It is not ok that we are are constantly being lied to and manipulated by our so called leaders. Their job is to represent us and to tell us the truth. Their job is to act on our behalf and solve problems in order to help the people. Their job is to fulfill the will of the people. So how pervasive is the lying and manipulation in the adversarial system of government? How vast is this paradigm of deception of manipulation? Let us examine all of it together.

CHAPTER 7

'The adversarial Courts'

Before we look at the courts adversarial system (17) I want to provide some context on deception and manipulation. If you sit down and talk with your best friend or a member of your family what is the unspoken expectation? You want the conversation to be real. You want the person your talking with to be honest. You don't want the person to deceive and manipulate you. How would one react to a best friend or family member saying and doing anything to twist the truth? How would one react if they felt that their best friend or family member was being totally manipulative? You would not like this at all generally speaking. Nobody likes to be lied to or manipulated constantly. You would eventually question the mental state of the lying manipulator. You might even wonder if this person constantly lying and manipulating you is some sort of narcissist (20)or worse. Anyone who always lies and manipulates is in some way just mentally off. Are many politicians narcissist? I'll leave that analysis to to reader.

So what happens in courts? Every person charged with a crime is entitled to due process or representation (21). This right to a fair trial is a great thing in principle. So you get arrested and charged with a crime and you have a trial with a jury of your peers. You have a judge, you have the prosecution and the defense. The prosecutor is a lawyer and the defense attorney is a lawyer. You have witnesses that can be called by both sides. The ultimate goal is supposed to be the revelation of the truth. The defendant must be guilty beyond a reasonable doubt.

Sounds fair enough but what is the paradigm of the adversarial system in the trial. If the defendant can't hire a great attorney they get a public defender (22). So the trial begins and the judge and jury will hear what? They will hear (arguments) (21). So now both sides, in my opinion, the prosecution and the defence will manipulate and twist the truth for their ultimate goal which we all know is winning. So the jury sits there and listens to two professional liars with the strict goal on both sides of winning the case. So the paradigm is one of deceiving the jury into believing either the prosecutor or the defense. So in essence the fate of the accused comes down to who was more successful in manipulating the opinions of the Jurors. Is this what the purpose of the court is? No not at all. The purpose of the court is to find the truth and execute justice based on the actual truth.

Yet this is a contest between two professional manipulators who openly attempt to coerce the very thoughts of the jurors. When I was much younger, I watched the OJ Simpson trial. OJ Simpson hired what was called the dream team of lawyers (23). He had the money to do this so he did. This team of lawyers so effectively manipulated the jury that OJ Simpson was found innocent. Everybody knew that OJ had commited murder. Yet these lawyers in the adversarial system lied so well to the jury that justice was not served.

I was watching a program on Investigation Discovery recently that just astonished me to the core. A man (Efren Saldivar) (24) who was working as a male nurse in a hospital was suspected by a coworker of killing patients. The accuser had no proof but he decided to report his suspicions to hospital management. Hospital management looked into it and came back to the accuser and advised him that had no evidence of wrongdoing and just left the issue alone. Eventually the accuser tipped off a couple of police detectives of his suspicions and pleaded with them stating "you have to do something about this guy". "I am positive he is killing patients but I can't prove it". So the police interview everyone in the hospital relevant to the investigation. The police arrive at a dead end because there is no proof and of course there are no victims. So after a while the police rolled the dice and ask the suspect to in for an interview.

During the interview the detective asks the suspect if he would be willing to take a polygraph test to clear him as a suspect. The suspected Killer says "I don't think that would be a good idea, I don't think I would pass the test". So the detective asks, why would you fail the test? The suspect replies, "I have suffocated patients". So the detective asked, how did you suffocate them? The killer replies "I gave them a paralytic drug that caused their body to shut down and the lungs just slowly stop working and the person is eventually asphyxiated". The detective then asked the killer how many patients he killed? The killer says "I stopped counting at 16 or 18". The detective asks him, well how many people would you estimate that you killed? The killer says, "around 150". So here we have a full blown confession from a killer who killed 150 people in a horrible cruel and brutal way.

So the Police place him under arrest for Murder. So now the police are allowed to hold him for 48 hours while they make their case based on the evidence. This is because a confession is not enough to convict him because the confession may have been coerced. So these detectives don't sleep for 48 hours trying to come up with a victim of the crimes or other evidence that will hold water in court. The detectives fail to come up with any victims of a crime or any direct evidence of what this killer confessed. The detectives call the District Attorney and they explain the situation regarding this monster. The District Attorney tells them the confession is not enough. So the killer walks right out the door after 48 hours. Eventually they exhume about 20 people who died while this monster was at work and they find the paralytic drug in these victims. They also kept him under surveillance while this was all happening. The hospital decided to fire him after he was initially arrested. The killer was arrested again and was found guilty in court.

So why did the District Attorney cut this monster loose? He did it because he is all to aware of the adversarial system in the courts. He knew that the defence attorney would eviscerate the case in court by arguing that you have a victimless crime and no direct evidence in my opinion. The only direct evidence was possibly a coerced confession (25). The case would be thrown out of court and the killer would roam free. In what universe is any of this an effective system of justice? We justify this in the name of protecting the due process afforded to the accused. This is the direct result of the adversarial system paradigm in the courts. A confession is not evidence? Thus far I have spent time writing about the problems to expose them. What about the solutions?

What would a non adversarial paradigm in courts look like? Why would it be better, and what on Earth can be changed to fix this system of deceptive manipulation in the courts? Let's start with the real case I just shared with you. I spent my entire career solving problems. We probably all agree with the fact that the accused criminals are entitled to due process. After all innocent people do end up in prison and we need to do everything we can to prevent this. However the system has gone amuck, so far, that a confession is not enough evidence to convict. One reason for this is that the police use interrogation techniques that can go on for 20 hours in which the suspect on occasion eventually breaks down and they actually become so confused that they end up believing that they actually did do it. In some cases people have confessed just to make the interrogation stop (25). So this is a simple fix. Every interrogation room needs to have audio video cameras on both sides of the table. With this a judge lawyer or jury can see and hear the whole interrogation from both sides of the table. That would allow the confession to become evidence of the crime. It will be obvious if the person accused was broken down to the point of confusion required to confess to an uncommitted crime.

This fix however is just regarding due process.It does not address the actual problem of the adversarial deception paradigm in the court system. For that we need an entire non adversarial system of justice in every court. So how on earth do we structure this system while preserving things like due process and the evidence? What about the lawyers and the judge and the jury? What about the presentation of evidence to the jury? How can all of this be done in a non adversarial way? How can we eliminate the manipulation of the jury by the prosecutor and the defence attorney? How do we prevent the OJ dream team (23) scenario in which the best lying lawyers get a murderer off the hook like magicians?

Sometimes the solutions to problems lie in simplistic structural changes to create a new and better paradigm. If the problem is the manipulation and deception of the jury we must remove the manipulators and there lies from the process completely. So how do we do this? We keep the Judge. The judge's job is to oversee the trial and keep the lawyers from going too far. So what is the goal of the jury? They get manipulated for the entire trial and they go into deliberation and try to agree on the guilt or innocence of the accused. They know the definition of the crime and it must be proven beyond a reasonable doubt in order to come to a guilty or innocent verdict.

So we replace the lawyers with what we can call a presenter. The judge will advise the Jury of the definition of the crime and what it means to deliberate the case. This includes the standard we already have that the crime must be proven beyond a reasonable doubt. The Police and the Prosecutor will amass the evidence in both written form and provide both physical and video evidence to the jury and the defence will do the same. All witnesses on both sides will submit written or video statements that the jury will have access to. Once all of the information for the case is compiled, a non influential and impartial Presenter will come in and simply provide the Jury with all of the information in the case. The Presenter will be completely devoid of opinion and will only be allowed to present the information to the jury.

This includes all witness statements, all evidence of every kind and the jury will be provided a file to each juror outlining everything the Presenter has presented which must be written in a way that is devoid of influence and manipulation of any kind. Anything that is slanted beyond the level of impartial information will be rejected by the Judge and sent back to the person who wrote it for correction. It will not be disallowed and removed from the evidence because all evidence must be available without exception. Once the Jury has been educated about the definition of the crime by the judge and presented with all of the impartial information of the case they will simply go into deliberation to reach a verdict.

In this system the Jury will be the influence to each other based strictly on the information. Their only function is to reach a verdict of guilt or innocence beyond a reasonable doubt. The lawyers and the defendant don't even appear in court. The defendant can submit a statement or not to the jury in writing or in the form of video on the advice of his or her attorney. When the Jury reaches a verdict the accused will stand before the court and hear the verdict. The jury will give an opinion to the judge based on sentencing guidelines for the crimes and the judge will sentence the accused based on the crime and the circumstances that warrant a light or severe sentence.

So what will this paradigm shift accomplish? A trial will be changed from a contest of the best manipulating lawyers swaying the jury. It will become a simple examination of the facts by an impartial jury that has nothing to win or lose. In all reality this would be much more fair for the accused and the victims of crimes. It's a fair shake that is the same for everyone. It eliminates adversarial manipulation of the jury and it would change the methods of police and lawyers since they would have to adapt to an impartial system. Police interviews would be all body cam recorded and used as evidence. Interrogations of suspects after being arrested would be structured by the police to never coerce an admission of guilt. The whole process would be recorded and fair for both the victims and the offenders. Errors like for forgetting to read an offender their rights will not be an avenue to throw a case out of court. All evidence will be revealed and the Officer who made the mistake will be fined or disciplined in some way. Every piece of information will be accepted by the court. Mistakes made in the case will be dealt with by either the Judge or the supervisor of the person who made a mistake in the collection of evidence. Any other technically that removes evidence from ever being allowed will be gone Every single piece of information relevant to the case will always be allowed . So with this non adversarial paradigm shift we eliminate lies and manipulation and the truth prevails and justice will be upheld more effectively in a system of truth and honesty.

Jury selection is part of a trial. I think the Judge should select the jurors personally, this is because a Judge is an expert on not being manipulated by lawyers. The Jury should be as diverse as possible. The law however should be a demand on the Jury that it embraces impartiality and only looks at the evidence to determine Guilt, innocence, or even a deadlock. Another option is to allow the defence and the prosecution have the ability to choose half of the jurors each. I don't care about the defence or prosecution interviewing potential jurors because they are not really manipulating these people they are just getting a feel if the person will lean in there direction. If it's done on both sides equally you have a fair mix of jurors. In the end it still needs to be established that the juror will be impartial and base findings on the evidence and all witnesses in the case.

A bench trial is a different animal entirely (26). A bench trial is simply a trial in which we have no jury at all. The Judge is the jury and these cases are (for the most part) used in lower level crimes. In spite of the fact that a Judge generally can not be manipulated by a lawyer due to the Judges complete knowledge of every game a lawyer will play. The Judge should also have the case information presented to him by a Presenter. Why? We need to be consistent in a non adversarial system. The Judge would probably appreciate not having to listen to the lawyers nonsense. So in these cases the Judge is simply provided with all of the information and all information is exempt from exclusion from the trial. The non exemption of evidence or witnesses or any information relevant to the truth must be included for the sake of finding the truth which is imperative to the finding of the 'whole truth' and the execution of justice in my opinion.

With regard to the Supreme Court of the United States (27). This (as you know) is the highest court in the United States. It has nine Supreme Court Justices who engage in deciding cases based on the United States Constitution and existing legal precedence. These Justices are all charged with the task of not allowing political affiliation or personal opinions to influence the findings they reach. They all say that they operate in a purely non partisan manor devoid of personal beliefs. This begs the question in my opinion, why do both the Democrats and the Republicans attempt to move Heaven and Earth to get either liberal or conservative Justices on the Supreme Court? The answer is pretty obvious in my mind. The Justices on the Supreme Court in this deceptive Adversarial System of Government (17) have clear agendas on every issue from Abortion to Gun control and every other major national issues.

So how do they get away with this? It's because of the fact that anything at all can be verbally presented to (feel) like it is justified and that it is the truth. This fact is not a paradigm but it is clearly illustrated by the aforementioned JonesTown Massacre (18). Nine hundred people were absolutely convinced that they should commit suicide. One of the main reasons I am writing this is to show people the importance of being able to think for themselves. People need to adopt an attitude that they are unwilling to be manipulated in there thought process. We all need to learn and (decide) to think for ourselves in all matters both personal and political. Can people choose to learn to think for themselves and form their own opinions in all things? They most certainly can. When it comes to the manipulative adversarial system of government (17) it is crucial that the masses form opinions on every issue one at a time. If your just going along with one party or another you are just 'drinking the Kool Aid' as we discussed earlier.

As I stated in the introduction I'm not generally interested in one party or another. What I am interested in is forming an intelligent opinion on each individual issue. I will share one of my opinions of a controversial subject as an example of independent and original thought. Gun control is something that one can just say I am for it, or I am against it, based on my political party. Gun control is a complicated issue in my opinion. The bases of the gun control issue being pushed in my opinion is because of what we call mass shooters or active shooters. What kind of guns do these mass shooters tend to use? The so called "assault rifle" or the so called "weapons of war" being sold to Americans. So are these actual weapons of war? In my opinion based on facts they are not weapons of war. They look the same but an AR-15 in the military is now called an M-4. This M-4 has a selector switch that allows the weapon to fire one round each time you pull the trigger. The second option is a three round burst where you fire three rounds when you pull the trigger. Then finally you have the option to select fully automatic machine gun fire. You as a citizen can not buy this M-4 weapon of war. You can however buy one that fires one round each time you pull the trigger (28). So we can clearly observe that you can not buy a weapon of war. So calling the AR-15 a weapon of war is a manipulative lie in the form of your average political manipulative speaking point.

Background checks seem quite reasonable to me. We can't have violent felons or the potentially violent mentally ill members of our society owning guns. I feel that this is a matter of Public Safety. I must ask myself if we eliminate these weapons in society and ban them, will it solve the problem of mass shootings? The facts tell me that it won't stop anything at all. In the Virginia Tech shooting, the shooter killed 32 people and injured 6 with two handguns.(He used a Glock 9mm pistol and a .22 caliber pistol made by Walther (29). This is relevant because these two pistols are not weapons of war and in fact they are not remotely what one would consider high power weapons. Then I must look at the fact that mass shootings are covered by the media as the exclusive reason for banning so called assault rifles. The media does not cover the fact that in Chicago you see 40 to 60 people shot every weekend and this also happens in many major cities (15).

Many of these shootings are gang and or drug related. So what do they use in Chicago? They use assault weapons like the AR-15 and the AK-47. But do we actually believe that these criminal gang members bought these weapons at the local gun store? They bought them on the black market (which already exists) (30). Many of these weapons are illegal because they are fully automatic and are in fact weapons of war. These weapons of war are being fired on people in Chicago which is a gun free zone. So we have an actual example of gun control not working at all. Not even the Police can destroy this black market of weapons that supply criminals with guns. In the end I believe that the problem lies in the behavior of the people. In our advanced civilization we have people killing each other on the streets every day. Every so often we have some deranged individual go into a school or other crowded places to kill as many people as they can. I can't embrace gun control because I have examined all of the information and it is clear to me that it will not work. I can assure you that in the end people will find a way to kill if they are determined to kill. So the problem lies in the behavior of some of the people. In order to change this the people must change. Gun control will not solve the problem of murderous and evil behavior. We can talk about the people later as we move forward. My point in this is to illustrate the idea that each issue must be examined individually. Each citizen should be looking at all of the information and basing their outlook on all of the information regardless of political party. It's simply an embrace of investigating information to establish original thought in the search for truth.

Now we will return to the Supreme Court (27) which will ultimately decide the issue of gun control. It would seem given the political bias of the Supreme Court that gun control will in fact not happen. Our three pillar system of government is supposed to provide checks and balances for each branch of government. So what branch of Government is responsible for placing checks and balances on the United States Supreme Court? It would seem they are pretty much operating independently. The Justices are appointed for life. I'm sure we have oversight mechanisms in courts, lawyers can be disbarred but what about corrupt Supreme Court Justice? They can be impeached by Congress for "bad behavior". Bad Behavior is a matter of personal interpretation by the Congress in my opinion.

These Supreme Court Justices are very partisan. Take Ruth Bader Ginsburg as an example. She in my opinion would probably rather die than retire and allow President Trump to seat another Supreme Court Justice. She is 86 years old, has had several bouts with severe cancer and other health problems (31). One might think she would retire and enjoy the remaining time she has. She is seemingly convicted by her conscious to remain in the Job for the sake of her partisan views as a liberal. I can respect this in the existing system but the existing system needs to change.

The Supreme court likes to appear to be separate from the political system. They always claim they will put their personal views aside and they will not even allow cameras into the court. In a non adversarial system without manipulation they need to eliminate arguments from lawyers as well. They like every other court should have the information presented to them. However, they won't need it explained by the Presenter like a jury. I'm sure they can examine the evidence and come to a conclusion in their findings. But they must be operating on a completely objective level. The Congress will be responsible for examining there findings and if they show a pattern of partisan politics in the findings they will be impeached by the Congress. All justice must be completely based on the information at all times. The courts will be houses of truth and not platforms for liberal or conservative agendas. The goal is to make a system that forces honesty just like our current system forces freedom and the rights of the people in this so called advanced civilization we live in.

CHAPTER 8

'The Adversarial Congress'

As I wrote earlier the Legislative Branch are the lawmakers in the House of Representatives and the Senate. This pillar of the three pillars are completely adversarial and completely deceptive and completely manipulative. As I mentioned earlier, our founding fathers adopted the adversarial system in my opinion right out of the Roman Republic as a leftover paradigm. Since I was a child I can recall hearing so many people expressing frustration with the Congress. They said over and over, "I can't stand the Congress, they are useless. They never get anything done, all they do is argue and tax us to death!" These are valid complaints and they are true.

There is much more than this to look at in the present day. As I mentioned earlier, they are allowed to be paid off by lobbyists and what is for sale? These lobbyists (9) pay them campaign contributions and buy influence for either their company or their cause. The lobbying ranges in everything from the Tobacco Industry, the National Rifle Association and huge corporations like Exxonmobil. This single fact that Senators and Members of the House are bought and paid for makes them completely unworthy to serve the will of the people. They are corrupt and these big money donors will spare no expense in wining and dining these Congress people. They are treated like Kings and Queens and I am quite certain our elected representatives like this very much. It must be so invigorating to be given this massive status and the inevitable power trip high that comes along with it.

But lobbyists (9) are not the main problem. Some people believe that the Lobbyist (9) are the biggest problem of all. They say just get rid of the Lobbyists and it will fix the Congress. The Lobbyist are just a symptom of the greater disease of this adversarial congress. The debating in congress is an argument between the two parties in our system being the Democrats and Republicans or the Liberals and the Conservatives. We also have the emergence of Progressives now. These are liberals in the Democratic Party that take their politics as far to the left as possible (32). These politicians are not actually interested in doing the will of the people and actually get things done. They fancy themselves idealist of their own perspective political philosophies.

The Republicans are sort of the type A personalities in my opinion that cling to religion and basic old school family values and seem to portray a common sense approach to a world view. They are pro-gun, anti abortion, pro big business, pro small business, and advocate for smaller government and lower taxes. There is much more but you get the general idea. The Democratic Party philosophy in my opinion is one of being the party of the people while the evil Republicans only care about big business. These are the politicians that project the idea that they actually care about the people and take care of the poor in a sort of self righteous delusion. They operate under the assumption that they are the smartest and most enlightened people in the room. They assume that the highly educated members of our society are the ones who really understand the

Democratic philosophy in it's intellectual superiority. They are anti gun, pro abortion, pro taxation and want bigger government. There is much more in the seperate party philosophies but you get the basic idea.

So each party has its own philosophy, why is that a problem? The problem is that they go out of there way to bring over three hundred million people to adopt these so called philosophies. If you take a closer look at the liberal philosophy you run right into what is known as political correctness (33). This is how you the citizens are supposed to think. It is what you are and are not allowed to say, it is what is and what is not allowed to be believed. This is more than philosophy. This is a system of defining morality for the masses in my opinion and if you don't comply you will be issued a label. For example if you are only for traditional marriage you are a homophobic person. If you have a problem with the Islamic Religion you are an Islamophobe. The list and labels go on and on. So now what you have coming from your elected representatives is nothing less than a pseudo religion. You must believe what they believe to be accepted you must comply with their code of morality or you are an unenlightened moron. How did we get here? Is this what the founding fathers had in mind? But the most important question with this whole mess is one simple question. Is all of this supposed to be part of their jobs as our elected representatives? How is this massive moral and mental manipulation filled with lies that we all consume a government of for and by the people? It is most definitely not.

Over the hundreds of years of the adversarial system of deception and lies the government has transformed into a group of arguing preachers who so wish to manipulate and control the masses. They even take the liberty of teaching us right from wrong. This was never their job and it never will be. But that's the existing paradigm in the advancement of our country and modern civilization. This system and it's paradigms also exists in every other Democratic country for the most part. So once again we need a solution that removes the lies, manipulation and divisiveness of this adversarial system. They fail to get things done for the people because they are so adversarial and corrupt that the needs, wants and priorities of the people are never even realised. In fact they decide what issues are important to the people. I thought that was our job. Speaking of Jobs it would seem that Congress has given themselves the best jobs in the world.

They work around 140 days per year. You work around 250 days per year on average (34). One would think that people in such an important job would at least work a normal schedule as the American People do. So we have a government body that works less than half of a work year. When they are working they fail to get things done and we all just accept this as normal. They in the past also liked to hold late night votes (off of the television) to vote themselves a big salary raise. Recently this has stopped. They unlike most people get a full pension (35) for working half of a year. Nobody in congress is required to be on Obama Care. All of this should be one of the first things that gets changed under a new system. We need congress to work all year to get the peoples work done. They should use our healthcare system and pay copays at the Doctor's office and get reasonable and decent pay and sick days and vacation time.

When a politician manipulates us it has its own word since the idea of us being manipulated is part of the paradigm. The word is 'rhetoric' here is the definition of rhetoric (36).

Language designed to have a persuasive or impressive effect on its audience, but often regarded as lacking in sincerity or meaningful content. (Translation in my opinion, manipulation lacking truth and sincerity or simple useless lies.)

This is what we the people consider the normal course of business from our elected officials. How do we fix this problem? We need once again to remove the ability of the politicians to lie to us and manipulate us. This can be done by eliminating rhetoric and the infighting of parties that we call debate in our system of government. How do we do this? We simply give the power to the people. We simply set up a democratic online polling system. Then we eliminate the debate system of arguing in congress. So in essence the job of the elected representative is to no longer to debate party politics. So the people of say New York go online in a federal website on the smartphone or PC and cast a vote on each of the issues that the people consider relevant. Each State in the country does this on every issue before congress. This voting goes on for say two weeks or a month if needed for one or multiple issues and then the vote is closed.

The elected member of Congress then stands up and says "The People of New York vote Ya or Na". And that is that. This process continues through every state and the law is either passed or failed. Laws passed will still have to be signed by the President and if the law presents some kind unlikely problem or threat to national security it can be vetoed (37). After a veto the law will be adjusted to compensate and the people will vote again.) So in this vast paradigm shift we are eliminating the Roman relic of the Adversarial System of Government (17). No more rhetoric no more debates no more philosophy and pseudo religious influence and no political correctness.

We the people become a nation of the people by the people and for the people. What I envision is, the Congress will also provide a long list of issues that can be considered by the people. We will vote online to establish a priority list. This can be tallied by the highest percentages of prioritization of the issues by the people and the issues will be taken up by the people in the selected order of priority. So in this system everything is simplified and the job of the politicians will be to speak the people's vote in congress and they will still conduct all of their other duties in their perspective committees like the intelligence committee, the ways and means committee and all of the rest. What we don't want is to be manipulated in any way regarding the issues by the government. This begs the question of party opinion being provided to the people of the two party system. The elected representatives will be charged with the task of providing either a written or video statement of impartial opinion. For example the Senator from Texas will post a video to the people on gun control. As it stands today he or she would be completely pro gun. The Senator would be required to offer a wide ranging impartial look at the entire issue and list many perspective points of view ranging from ultra liberal to moderate to ultra conservative. If the Senator fails to be impartial the Senator will subject to impeachment or some form of disciplinary action.

In my opinion the reason we need all sides of the issue in every State is because every state has every type of voter living in it. They all need to be equally represented in spite of the majority of Texans being Republicans. Now how are the issues going to be debated? The congress no longer has the power to manipulate the people or use rhetoric. They only speak the will of the people and provide impartial information much like the presenters in the court system. The people are the ones with power, so if people want to discuss, debate or argue an issue then let them argue. This is not an adversarial system of government it is the people not the congress debating the issues. Ultimately it's kind of like Facebook, everyone has the right to an opinion but people generally will reject online criticism and vote their own conscience. So why allow people to debate at all? Two reasons, people will always argue, it is part of human nature for us to reason with and argue with each other. Secondly, the people must continue to have freedom of speech. We don't want to eliminate discussion we only want to remove the paradigm of the adversarial system of Government. The people discussing or arguing issues does not have the same effect as a government manipulating and lying to the people and pushing belief systems down our throats. We the people will in fact likely become much more informed and intellectual as the voice of the country. In time you may see parties simply become irrelevant as I see them and things will just be decided on one issue at a time.

So what about the system being hacked? I am quite certain that a secure system can be established. You may need to mix the online system with a final telephone call to cast the vote. For all I care we could make a social media platform on the federal level. You could receive a sort of second social security number as a voter. This voter number will not be shared and in order to sign in to the system you will have to go through a validation of identity process. But basically I am saying that this can be done in this technological age of things like facebook and online banking, shopping and socializing on the internet. This system should only be accessed by American citizens of voting age.

Does this sound like an advanced civilization to you in comparison to the embarrassing zoo we live in now? It sounds like it to me. In all reality, this makes the people themselves a fourth branch of the government. After all this is a matter of checks and balances. It's simply time for the people to speak and it's time for the politicians to listen to us. There would be other benefits in the new system that we will be positive side effects of the new system as it advances through time.

CHAPTER 9

'The Adversarial
Executive Branch'

The office or the President is a crucial office to examine. Let's define what a President really is in my opinion. The President is the most powerful man or woman in the world. The President is the Commander and Chief of the entire United States military, the most powerful military in the world. The President has the power to engage in warfare with or without the permission of congress. The President has the authority to engage in a multiple types of executive orders with executive privilege. The President has what is known as the so called bully pulpit. Translation, the President has the loudest voice in the country and his or her words yield the most influence over the people. The President has the right to veto laws. The President carries the so called football or the Nuclear Codes as they say. This means the President could launch a nuclear attack on an enemy country.

This is a lot of power to say the least. Does the President manipulate the people with Rhetoric? Sure they do. They have press conferences and use rhetoric on a regular basis and they disparage members of the opposite party. With the exception of President Trump most Presidents are as fake as any other politician. One could argue or assume that Trump was elected because in spite of all of his faults he does not act like a typical politician. The people either love him or hate him because he is not afraid to be real. He will attack anyone in the government and lie to the government for his own benefit. He will attack the media and tell them on live television that they are fake news and they should be ashamed of themselves. He calls them all a disgrace right to their faces.

Yet when he holds a rally he becomes 'real' and speaks to the people with a tone of common sense truth and claims with huge banners "Promises made Promises Kept". He is like an entertainer and his supporters love him for it no matter what he does. And to be fair he has thus far done a lot of the things he promised. What he hasn't been able to do has been blocked by the congress. One example would be the wall on the Mexican border. He can't get all of the funding but he is still finding money and building as much of it as he can. Trump draws fifty thousand people to his rallies. Why? Because he connects with people and he tells it as he sees it with no manipulation and no rhetorical manipulation. He's an actual real person and not a politician. This amazing phenomenon of Trump winning is a sort of evidence that the people sense that they are being manipulated and lied to under the adversarial system of Government. We all know either consciously or unconsciously that we are being lied to and the people finally got fed up with it all. So in essence the People told the government to piss off and elected the opposite of a politician for all the reasons I'm writing about here. Again this my personal opinion.

The Trump phenomenon will end at some point and we will get another rhetorical liar who has more power than any other person on the planet. Is this massive power simply too much for one person? I believe it is. The Supreme Court (27) has nine

Justices not one. Yet the Supreme office of the Executive Branch is one person with one Vice President. So why not establish a Presidential or Executive Council? Let's say you have a seven member office of the Presidency. And let's say that we need to have actual qualifications to be a part of Executive Council of the Presidency. Unlike Congress the President is a sort of manager of the United States. He like any manager is on call 24-7. The President can at any time be confronted with a national emergency and must act in a timely manner in some cases. So this council I am talking about will have to do the same thing in the case of an emergency. So in order to guarantee that issues are handled correctly you must have a leader of this council that is empowered to make a final decision in the case that an agreement or consensus can't be reached. This person can be called The Chief Executive of the council. Under a system of non adversarial government the President would not really need to attack the congress in back and forth rhetoric since rhetoric will be gone in congress. This executive council will be speaking as a leadership group which is a vastly different dynamic than one person at the very top. The Executives can be called for example Mr. Executive or Mr. Chief Executive or Executive Smith. We don't need a Vice President with this council in place. The Executives could multitask Executive Branch priorities like visiting other countries and hosting other countries. All major decisions must reach a consensus of the council with the final say as I said going to the Chief executive when issues are deadlocked.

In today's system you don't really have to have any specific qualifications to run for the Office of the President. Right now we have a local mayor running for the Democratic Nomination to run for President. So what do want and need in a President with regard to qualifications? One issue is the fact that the President is the Commander in Chief of the military (38). I think it would be wise to have the Chief Executive of the council being required to have served in the military. Preferable in a position of higher rank. This is not to discount members of the military in lower ranks. However, the Chief Executive would be dealing with Generals in decisions making. We need someone who understands the military to be it's Commanders in Chief.. The other council members should have some form of leadership experience. But what I think we should really want in this council are the smartest people in the room and people with serious life experience and wisdom.

What people seem to want in the present day is the person with the most charisma. President Obama had political experience, but the minute I saw him speak for the first time I told everyone I knew that Obama would become President. I knew this because he spoke like Dwane Johnsen other known as The Rock from professional wrestling. He spoke with a massive amount of Charisma. He inspired the dreams of the people and promised a wonderful free healthcare system that would satisfy everyone and you would be able to keep your doctor and insurance company somehow. Like all or most Presidential candidates he made a gigantic list of promises that could never be kept in all reality. He was competing against Hillary Clinton who has very little charisma. So to close out the thoughts on the Presidency, I feel that we need a non adversarial council of the office of the Presidency. It would have a leader in place to assure emergency management and make final decisions in deadlock situations. So we either get a council agreement or final decision by the Chief. The Chief executive and all members of the council should address the media in news conferences and the Chief executive should give the State of the Union Address with the other executives standing behind him or her in solidarity. A council of seven will increase the odds of balanced decision make the efficiency of operations increase exponentially.

CHAPTER 10
'The Adversarial Elections'

The Electoral College (39) is a hot button issue that is both confusing and seems to be against the simple idea of 'one person one vote'. The best defense of it that I have read is the idea of preventing what is called regionalism or sectionalism (40). Regionalism is the concern that the States with the highest population totals would be the only ones that were campaigned in. The rest of the smaller States would be irrelevant in the election process. So the founding fathers in essence placed a check and balance on us the people. States get the same number of electoral votes as they have members in congress. In researching the electoral college it seems that the Founding Fathers were concerned about the formation of factions of some sort forming that would make the election process corrupt and unfair. It is in the constitutions 12th Amendment (41) I'm not clear on the exact concerns they had. One thing to keep in mind with this decision they made is the time period they were in when these decisions were made.

This was before we even had electricity or light bulbs. Things back then were different, we had no modern technology including systems of communication beyond a messenger. So the idea of factions forming was under a paradigm that people might be forming up groups that the government wasn't even aware of. So to ensure a fair election, perhaps this was necessary at the time to prevent what they considered some kind of corrupt manipulation of the elections. Groups forming and engaging in corrupt practices to sway people in there own favor and to benefit themselves. I can only speculate on the reasons but I'm sure the Founding Fathers at that time had the best of intentions during this historical time frame. On the other hand, if for whatever reason this notion of regionalism or as some call it 'sectionalism' becomes an issue. The people could simply put the electoral college back into affect. If the people are in charge much more will get done by congress. The current congress takes far too long to get the job done. Under a congress of the people things will get done quickly. This would be true progress.

So I guess the intentions are good but many people think this should end. While we may not have this so called regionalism we do see Presidential candidates placing focus on the big States. For example, Florida, Texas, California and New York since they have the most electoral college votes. We also see an extreme interest in so called swing states that could go either way. So if the idea of the Founding Fathers was to prevent corruption of the election by making every State equally relevant, the truth is that some States are more important than others. What are the effects of the adversarial system of government on the election? Within the paradigm of lies and manipulation we see hundreds of millions of dollars being spent on one thing. Campaign financing (42),that is the use of TV and other venues to manipulate you into believing in these candidates so they can gain your vote. In fact, in the present day a big part of a candidate's success level throughout the process is the amount of money they have to influence you. So if the goal is to end adversarial lying manipulation and rhetoric, this is certainly going on in the elections.

Another part of these adversarial election systems are the debates. We basically see a bunch of people on a stage disparaging each other and making grandiose promises to the American People. For example we have the Green New Deal (43) and Medicare For All (44) being advertised as a definite reality if you elect Bernie Sanders or Elisabeth Warren in the year 2020. This cost is 130 trillion dollars over ten years. Even the other Democrats are saying that this will never be passed into law and yet people will still believe it, and some will go to rallies and cheer these people on like the true believers that they are.

For my entire adult life I have listened to Presidential candidates making false promises of great and massive things that never happen. Most people are aware of this and yet it is just part of the accepted norm in our political system. In essence this electoral process is all about the person with the most money to effectively manipulate you. In local elections politicians don't have a hundred million dollars so they are reduced to putting red or blue signs on the side of the road. You may even see one with a group of supporters waving to you in the center of town as you drive past to gain your vote even though you have no idea who this person is.

What can a non adversarial election system look like and how could it work? Once again we must remove the existing paradigm. Money for starters must be removed from the process. Once that is gone we must place all candidates on an even playing field. This won't be about rhetoric or false promises that inspire the masses with false hopes of a better life. This will be a job interview. Since in our new system we will have no more debate or rhetoric in congress the same thing will apply to the elections this should include State and local elections as well in my opinion. If we have a federal website that we access to vote, this website can also provide an even playing field for prospective candidates. For example, all of the candidates can make a video that is allowed to be a certain time length. In the case of an executive council, teams of seven candidates can produce videos and explain to the people on the federal website why they should get the job. In the absence of rhetoric they can all explain their qualifications from leadership skills to life experience and how they would handle an emergency situation. They should also provide all of the information about themselves and their beliefs. We want to know that they are impartial, qualified, full of life experience and intelligent wisdom.

We are not interested in charisma, these people are not Hollywood actors. We are interested in the smartest and wisest people in the room. With this we will eliminate all debates which eliminates all rhetoric and all manipulation. Every candidate gets the same forum to apply for the job and big money will have no influence on anything. No more billionaires or huge corporate donors dishing out campaign contributions in exchange for future favors. This is very important because the Presidential Council and all members of Congress will only be motivated to do the will of the people. As it stands now it would seem they are all indebted to donors and lobbyists. One nice thing about an online voting site is that a series of votes could be held based on the interview videos from the candidates. We will eventually widdle down the nominees for the election until we reach two competing candidates.

With everyone being elected based on job interview videos on an even playing field we create a massive paradigm shift. The entire country will be subject to the same amount of so called campaigning on this website. So now every State receives identical amounts of information and influence by the candidates.

We therefore will no longer have any need for either campaign finance which corrupts the politicians and we will have no need whatsoever for any type of electoral college. We all receive the same information nationally. So this is a simple side effect of the new non adversarial paradigms. So it's one person one vote and the so called 'popular vote' wins the election. My main point here is that paradigms have consequences, this is a positive one, and that in the end is the general idea. Positive new paradigms replacing old damaging relic paradigms.

What if the people are afraid the election will be hacked by Russia or some other enemy? Then perhaps we vote the issues online and the Presidential and MidTerm elections in the traditional way. The only difference needs to be the time frame of the election. Have you ever found it strange that we get one Tuesday every four years to vote? I sometimes wonder if they don't want people to vote. Regardless of the reason for it we should have the entire month of November to go to the polls. As it stands now the majority of voters just don't bother to go out and vote. In my opinion if we changed the system in a way that empowers the people and it has its own website we will see a dramatic increase in participation by the people. And as the generations pass and this all becomes part of public education it will increase more and more. The online voting system however is the best and most convenient way to go. We did manage to create a national website for Obama Care. I believe we can do the same for the non adversarial system of government. I have heard nothing about the Obama care website being hacked. If it can't be done today it can be done at some point in the future as internet security advances. But let us be real, we can do this now.

CHAPTER 11

'The Adversarial Media'

Over the course of time I have heard many people say "I don't watch the news it's all negative, it's depressing". This is true, yet some people seem to also love watching the news and seeing all of the arguing and wars. They watch terrorist attacks along with mass shootings and big stories about serial killers. As for me, I just want to know what is going on in my country and in the world. All of the negative information doesn't really depress me, the partisan arguing on the other hand is just annoying. So what does the news media fancy itself to be? You would think they would view their job as reporters to simply report the information to everyone. Maybe many years ago that was case.

The current media in my opinion actually fancy themselves to be a powerful branch of government whose job it is to place checks and balances on our government. They, like our politicians believe it is their job to educate the general public on what is in fact, reality. Depending upon which channel you watch you will receive a certain education by these great teachers of morality and political correctness or conservative values. Not only does the media teach us what to believe like a religion, the politicians use the media to broadcast their manipulation to match whatever rhetoric they are pushing at the moment.

We must have freedom of the press in my opinion. The media will however be in a whole new position with a non adversarial system of government. What will they have to report on? They can report what people voted on and what way the vote went. Since the politicians in Congress and the Office of the President will not be at verbal war between parties back and forth, things might get a little boring for the press.

They would still be able to discuss their own opinions from right to left but the politicians would not be going on the news to support or oppose it. So in addition, I believe the government website should offer a service to the people that provides what we can call the daily information. It's just the same things that the news is reporting with regards to international politics, national events, emergencies, natural disasters, terrorist attacks, mass shootings and all of the other stories being reported in the media. The difference is that it's not opinion based, it is simply the information about what happened. So for example when a mass shooting happens they simply explain the event and it's details. We won't get a sermon on gun control or anti gun control at all. Just the information will do, we are smart enough to think about gun control on our own.

If you want to watch CNN go ahead but at least people will have an option that does not attempt to influence them. But I think with freedom of the press we will always have slanted talk shows that lean in both directions. The media may eventually shift to a less partisan presentation of the facts because that's the way there viewers will be thinking. A sort of media evolution to the new system of uninfluenced thinking. The media in its present state is lead by people who choose the priorities and assign what is reported based on either the liberal or conservative philosophy. The big national media outlets make a huge amount of money and they care about ratings. Rather you like

Wolf Blitzer or Shawn Hannity is not the issue. The issue is that the American People need to create their thoughts and philosophies and beliefs. If we want religion we can go to Church and be influenced by a Preacher or Priest or Rabbi or an Islamic Teacher or a Hindu Leader or whatever. That is actually their job. And they all teach one thing in common for the most part. God gave us free will to decide our own thoughts and actions. We can choose good and evil and everything else. So in closing out the media discussion, I think we should preserve freedom of the press with the hopes that they evolve to the non adversarial system. We need an impartial government provided video link that by law must be totally impartial and simply give the information without so much as a single tone of bias.

CHAPTER 12

The Adversarial
American People

I keep hearing the media use this term describing the American People. They say the country is 'polarized' (45). So what are they saying? It's simply the idea that we the people are divided into two separate groups opposing each other. That would seem to be the case in our current situation. When you look at the election results, especially over the say, the last 15 years. Entire States come down many times to a couple of thousand votes. How many times have we heard the media use the term 'too close to call'. We have recounts and Goerge W Bush VS Al Gore was so close it ultimately had to be decided by the Supreme Court after election and recounts and hanging chads kept the election contested for what felt like years at the time (46).

I have an opinion that this is actually evidence of the problems I'm seeing in the Adversarial system. The existing system of government and it's paradigms are like tentacles of influence that reach from the Government down to the States and down to the people themselves. This has been true in every culture throughout history. It was true in Sparta, it was true in Germany through two world wars and it was true in cannibalistic tribes in the amazon basin. So are we all just uneducated sheep? That may have been the case in the distant past when the majority of the common people received very little education. So what's the difference with us?

What I believe is that we are as the American people very educated smart people who are simply asleep to the paradigms we live under. When you are born and raised in a system hundreds of years old certain paradigms take hold of everyone. This book is a simple attempt to show you the reader a few paradigms that we seem to have just not recognised as problems. As I mentioned in the beginning, before the creation of this government of the people, the world never dreamed that there could be a paradigm excluding Kings Queens or Dictators. It took a revolution and a group of ingenious visionaries to invent our current system.

They only came up with this system, I believe, by questioning thousands of years of established paradigms. They took these assumptions and asked themselves and each other what can we do to set people free? They started looking at the idea that the people themselves could be the government. Then they had to develop this idea and anticipate every single thing that could go wrong and cause the people to lose their freedom based system. So the Constitution is a rule book that prevents everything they could think of that would destroy the freedom of the people. As a result we became the greatest country in human history and have been mimicked by many countries including England, the one we rebelled against. England still has a mock monarchy with kings and Queens as a matter of pride and tradition but they became a Democracy just like their former enemy.

People say in many cases that it is unwise to discuss politics and religion. These and many other issues can become arguments and even evolve to the level of verbal confrontations or in rare cases people will even fight over things physically. This is especially true when alcohol is involved. So what we see in our senior citizens is a tendency to keep things 'closer to the vest' as they say. They just don't talk about who they voted for or controversial issues. The younger people these days want to advertise everything they believe in this age of things like gender identity, LGBTQ rights and acceptance by all. And in college they have little safe spaces they go to in order to, I guess feel safe somehow. We have debates about transgender public restrooms and all manor of things that feel alien to the older generations. The sexual orientation of the individual is no longer a private matter, it is broadcasted from the rooftops and you will listen and you will call it morally correct unless you wish to receive a label of political incorrectness. That is the current state of things in the present and I'm not writing this to embrace or reject this. All of this is irrelevant to my purpose in writing this. People have the right to say what they want to say and do what they want to do. If they want to push it in your face it's their right and it's your right to handle it in any way you find appropriate. So one aspect of a polarized population as I mentioned earlier is the existence of two sides. So generally speaking people seem to assume under the current paradigm that they have two choices on just about every issue. You are either pro gay marriage or you are pro traditional marriage as a religious institution. And the list goes on and on. You are either pro this or pro that.

In essence you have been limited to two choices and the influencing factors are generally delivered to you by your political party and religious or non religious beliefs. So what about options three four and five or ten? Well that's just not how it works in the existing paradigm. Is life really that simple and are issues really that simple? Two choices for everything is a rather limited paradigm in issues that are so complex in nature. The better way to see things in my opinion is to observe all of the information on both sides and find other information beyond the two simple choices. So let's take a look at one of the most controversial and explosive issues in our time, abortion.

Some of you may be thinking, oh no, he's going to go there. Yes I am, however I am not going to talk about my own opinion of the issue at all. I am going to simply attempt to take a look at all of the information that exists on the issue that (I) would observe in making a truly informed decision. So within the existing paradigm we have two options pro-choice and pro-life. Democrats tend to be pro-choice and Republicans tend to be pro-life. So in defining pro-choice what are some of the connected assumptions in the paradigm in my opinion ? A woman has 're-productive rights', a woman has the right to choose 'what she does with her own body'. If we outlaw abortion we will go back to a barbaric time of back ally abortions with coat hangers. The pregnant female should not give birth if she is not ready to be a mother. The pregnant female should not bring a baby into a poverty situation. A pregnant woman should not give birth if the baby is going to be in a drug infested abusive and or broken household. The baby for whatever reason is better off not being born at all. An unborn child is a fetus object and not a person. And finally late term abortions and even post birth abortions are simply a choice of the woman controlling her body. Eliminating this appendage that is not a person but only an object to be discarded at the woman's discretion. This is not an issue of morality like religious morons preach, it's not a person at all. This abortion is what is right for me and I have every right to have it and it is perfectly fine on a moral level.

On the pro life side in my opinion, we have the idea that abortion is murder plain and simple. We are not in a position to play God. Have the child and give it up for adoption. Planned Parenthood is an abortion industry just looking make money and they sell fetal body parts on the open market. Abortion is an abomination in the eyes of God and nothing less than infanticide on a grand scale. The baby is a person at the moment of conception. Late term abortions are a sign of the 'culture of death' which will ultimately lead to euthanasia. What about the father of the baby, does he have a right to choose in this decision? A fetus is not a finger nail it is a person. And the list goes on and on.

So what other information can we look at with regard to abortion in an impartial way and what contradictions exist between the two sides taken on the issue? One thing rarely observed is the psychological effects of abortion. Science tells us that all women have maternal instinct and that they actually start bonding with the baby or fetus before birth. So on the one hand a women or sixteen year old will walk out of the abortion clinic saying I did the right thing, I did what I had to do. Yet unless she is devoid of emotion and maternal instinct in my opinion she will at some point be saying to herself "I killed my own baby". This is a known issue in the area of psychology and is of course argued on both sides of the issue (47) . So can we objectively say, planned parenthood should advise their customers of the long term potential psychological impacts of abortion? Planned Parenthood would find this bad for business in my opinion. But what about the law regarding the unborn? As it stands it is legal to get an abortion. It is also assumed that a fetus is not a person. Yet when a person murders a pregnant woman they are charged with the death of two people (48). This is a Federal Law called The Unborn Victims of Violence Act . This is not logical if the fetus is not a person. According to the law a fetus is not a person. Should a person be charged with murdering a non person? This happens in murder cases all the time. The killer gets two counts of murder when he or she kills a pregnant women.

If it is true that a fetus at any stage is a non person then the accused killer is being falsely charged and this is a total injustice being placed on the accused. If we are talking about the fetus as an unborn legitimate person, in that case, justice is being served and the unborn person has been murdered. Police regardless of their position on the abortion issue will find the murder of a pregnant woman quite disturbing and will view the killer of an unborn baby to be a particularly monstrous act. Only a monster would kill a pregnant woman. This is a second contradiction in the information. The last one is a matter of medicine. We all for the most part see these commercials on TV advertising medications. The drug companies by law must advise the public of the side effects of these medications in every commercial. I sometimes hear these side effects and wonder if I should go to the doctor at all. In this case I want to examine the fact that the commercials at times warn that the patient should not take the drug if the person is pregnant because the drug could harm an unborn baby. They don't warn against the drug damaging a fetal object. So again we see contradictions between the two definitions of a fetus.

When you boil this all down the question becomes, is a fetus a person or a non person? So what is the answer to this question under the current paradigms in the abortion issue? The answer to the question of is a fetus a person or a non person is a resounding both. It would seem that under our current system that if the baby is wanted by the pregnant woman and she plans to give birth we are dealing with an unborn person that can be murdered. If the woman does not wish to give birth and plans to abort the pregnancy then she is carrying a non human fetal object that can be removed as an appendage at any stage of pregnancy. This is all of the information I see on this issue. I'm sure I'm missing something, but what is the general point in this writing? My objective in writing this to show the importance of looking at every piece of information on both sides before forming an opinion on the perspective issue. I have no intent to sway you one way or another on abortion. That is your job, not mine. You have the right to form your own opinion. What I am saying however, is that issues are more complex than just the partisan viewpoints of each political party. Every issue needs a complete examination from both sides. I do this with every issue and some of my opinions are conservative, some are liberal and some are neither at all.

Our culture is in fact polarized in a way that is literally about 50/50 on each side. What are the odds of that happening if we are all engaging in independent original thinking? In the case of original independent thought by the masses it would be highly improbable that we would be split right down the middle. It would be 70/30 or 60/40 in my opinion. In a two party system with a paradigm on both sides that lie and manipulate how you think it becomes very likely to be split 50/50. We are participating in a system that is no more realistic than professional wrestling. When you see someone dropped on there head in pro wrestling they just shake it off and keep fake fighting. If you drop someone on their head in real life you will break their neck or kill them outright.

This idea of a non adversarial system in the of the areas I am discussing will have an effect from the top all the way down the system to the general population. Just as our current system does in having us polarized and full of division. I would imagine that the side effects would be positive. The people would be the ones who are thinking on a national level or it could be called, engaging in global thinking. We are all subject to influence regardless of whether we want to be or not. This divisive polarized 50/50 two party reality we live in is proof that the reality projected by our leaders has a vast influence on a population of 329,000,000 people(49). This also happens in every other country and culture. So we by proxy must evolve under a non adversarial system. The example of our leadership will not be adversarial or combative or manipulative. We the people will follow suit and become well educated thinkers and leaders ourselves. This would be an advancement of human civilization that will only increase and improve over time. Can we eliminate all of the evil that people do and change the darker parts of human nature? No we can't, but we can greatly reduce these tendencies and create a vastly more civilized intelligent culture.

CHAPTER 13
'Todays Visionaries'

Do I consider myself a visionary? Not really, I'm just a person who spent a lot of time looking at things and questioning everything. Eventually I saw these existing paradigms as problems that are invisible to most people. You the reader can define that in any way you choose but I don't want to call myself anything special. We are all equally special and the vast majority of us may never see their own vast potential. As I mentioned earlier, we are in an age in which most people are in possession of at least a basic education. In the distant past, most people could not even read or write. The average American is operating a smartphone, has a social media account and is plugged in to more information than ancient people could have ever imagined. So the potential of the public at large ranging from the wealthy to the poor have the ability to think on the level of an advanced civilization. The potential for this under our current paradigm is simply unrealized by most people. As I mentioned earlier we are asleep to paradigms that have existed for hundreds of years. If you change the paradigm the people will follow suit and we can all be visionaries in our time if we so choose.

So let's examine what the visionaries of this time are envisioning under our current adversarial systemic paradigm. In all reality I don't see to many incredible ideas coming from our leaders. We tried to help the people with a free healthcare system. It turned into a gigantic mess and many people pay more now then they did before the Affordable Care Act(50). The Congress actually passed this law before they read the actual bill. I find this so far beyond unacceptable that I don't know a word to describe it. How can they pass something this huge and this important without reading it first? Well it was over a thousand pages long for one thing. So a key issue in the current 20/20 election is healthcare. If Obama Care worked we would be all set, yet now we have a new problem to solve in this very broken healthcare system. So now they talk about this visionary idea of Medicare for all (44). This effort by the Democrats will as I mentioned earlier cost more money then we could afford to pass in congress. So when it comes to healthcare, in essence we have no solution or visionary idea on either side of the isle. I hear a lot of talk about making prescription drugs more affordable, yet they are not currently even explaining how this will be done.

When it comes to the huge climate change issue we have a visionary idea of a Green New Deal (43). This visionary concept revolves around the idea that if we make the United States carbon free we can save the planet from overheating. The problem with that is the simple fact that even if you managed to acquire a hundred trillion dollars to do this by some miracle it only fixes the United States. So what about China who uses more coal than the entire world and is expanding coal fired power plants as we speak (51). Then you have all of the third world countries in South America burning coal along with Russia and India. Then we have billions of vehicles all over the planet burning gas and 18 wheelers burning a lot of diesel fuel across the entire planet. Then we hundreds of thousands of commercial airline flights every week and of course we have cows excrement emitting carbon all over the world.

The young people in college and Bernie Sanders say we have nine years to fix all of this before it's too late and major cities will end up underwater (52). Those are Bernie's words on the campaign trail right now. So young people are literally in terror now because they think the world is going to end in their lifetime. So the current visionary plans from our leaders are just kind of a joke of sorts. I will offer this opinion. I have no faith in humanity going green any time soon on a global level. I do have faith in natural law however. The Earth has no problem cooling itself down. In 1883 Mount Krakatoa erupted and produced the loudest explosion in the history of the world which was heard around the entire world. It put so much ash into the Earth's atmosphere that the world was dim for four years and the Earth was cooled. So I don't worry too much about climate change. It is called Volcanic Winter (53) To quote George Carlin the comedian (who I'm not really a huge fan of) "This planet will shake us off like fleas".

Another visionary concept of the day is the idea that the United States becomes a Socialist Country (54). So we get a gigantic government system that takes everybody's money and gives out to everyone and we eliminate free market capitalism. Yet we watched Europe fall apart financially when they did this. Greece was a prime example. When the financial system collapsed and people's entitlements were taken away they had riots that went on for a long period of time. These protests were extremely violent with people attacking riot police with 4 or five foot sticks and molotov cocktails(55). Once you give the people a system of endless free stuff they will get used to it. When the money runs out and you take the free stuff away, the people will lose their minds. So in essence Socialism is a visionary idea being put forth with many examples of the failure of Socialism all over the world. Why would we want to do something that we know will fail? Well it's because young voters like the idea of free college and they love the idea of a revolution against big business. The politicians are making promises based on popularity regardless of effectiveness. Socialism will hopefully never become our system of government but at the moment it is being advertised to the voters as a great idea in spite of its historical failure. We can talk more about Capitalism moving forward.

The only other grand visionary idea I see is this notion of Globalism (56). This is the idea that we simply get rid of countries all together and perhaps establish a Democratic Free Planet. So as we heard President George HW Bush said "I see a thousand points of light, a new world order" (57). When he said this many years ago it actually alarmed a lot of people. People became frightened that some kind of massive world government was going to be formed whether we liked it or not. One of the biggest proponents of Globalism is the Billionaire George Soros(58). George Soros is an activist Billionaire who supports liberal causes and spends huge amounts of money trying to influence the direction of the country and the world for that matter. He is the subject of many many conspiracy theories (59).

People believe he's part of the so called Illuminati or some other secret society, he's accused of trying to run the world behind the scenes. I honestly can't give George that kind of credit and I don't believe the conspiracy theories about him. I tried to figure out where the origins of this globalism concept came from. In the end I actually believe that he and others simply heard the song written by John Lennon entitled imagine. They may have said "hey this guy is on to something". Some of the lyrics are "Imagine no possessions", "imaging no more countries", "nothing to kill or die for, a brotherhood of man". "You may say I'm a dreamer but I'm not the only one". "I hope someday you will join us, and the world will live as one". I you have never heard imagine, listen to it, it is an outline for globalism and world peace (60).

I say yes Mr. Lennon you are a dreamer. Not to speak ill of the dead, but this idea is impossible. So you erase all of the lines on the map and every country just goes along with this in the name of peace and love. Let's give it a look from my perspective. So we are going to tell Russia, China, North Korea, Saudia Arabia, Iran, Iraq and all these other countries that they should just abandon their sovereignty to join a new world order. Just in terms of Islamic Republics we would be asking them to abandon Sharia Law which is their religion based system of government demanded by the Prophet Mohammed. China wants to replace us as the largest superpower and Russia wants to reestablish the Soviet Union under Vladimir Putin. I don't wish to be sarcastic but I have to say, good luck with that George. Now if you somehow end up reading what I'm writing here Mr. Soros, you might want to start a grassroots movement with all of that money you use to build a better world.

So why are we lacking in wonderful visionary ideas in this highly technological stage of human history? Perhaps the reason is that we are gradually losing the propensity for original thought. As we have gradually become this polarized culture of rhetoric and adversarial manipulation we have stopped being visionaries as our founding fathers were. We are more concerned with how many likes we got on a facebook post than we are about our own health. Evidence of the lack of original thought can be seen in Hollywood. We still have some decent movies that come out, but we don't see very many epics coming out anymore. The biggest epics in the last ten or fifteen years have based on old comic books written by Stan Lee years ago or DC Comics using Batman and other comic books. Where is the

Stan Lee of today? I don't think we have one at the moment. Do we a modern day Mozart? Not that I know of.

So as we have advanced in technology and medicine and in things like the internet and the microchip and smartphones we seem to have reversed direction in the development of the person. Should we be much further along than we are? Think of it in these terms. We now have a global nuclear arsenal and yet our leaders still lie to us and manipulate us. People still argue and fight from the government to the population. How have human beings evolved to the next level in the same way our technology has? Human behavior has not evolved as much as we would like to believe. We should remember that it was only 70 years ago that we declared victory over Adolf Hitler and Nazi Germany (61). I am personally hesitant to assume that this sort of thing could not happen again. Because of this I think an advancement in humanity is actually overdue. But we can break that down later.

So one benefit of people waking up to a new paradigm of original thought and opinion in a non adversarial government of the people might be a renewal of original creative thinking. Then perhaps we can start producing visionaries in this country again. The biggest innovations we see come in the form of I-phones and video games. The next level of high resolution TV is the big new thing as we watch football on Sunday. Technology advances yet the system stagnates in its state of antiquity. Innovation on the corporate level is well financed, yet the individual inventor is limited to the next as seen on TV product. They don't want some revolutionary thing invented anymore, they seem to just be looking for the next Sham Wow or George Foreman grill in my opinion. So many things could be invented right now but never are. I can imagine land based hydroelectric power generation using tanks and heavy weights operating like huge syringes with enormous weights pushing water through a turbine filling the opposite tank using simple gravity 98 percent of the time to generate electricity the other two percent of the time hydraulics lift the weights. I can imagine a truck that melts snow using high pressure warm water and sucks the water into a huge tank and then dries the road as it passes over. But the secret to society inventing is a population of original visionary thinkers. If Thomas Edison were alive today he wouldn't be able to invent much of anything unless he was working for some major corporation like Apple or the like.

CHAPTER 14

'The Financial System'

So now that we have untangled the circus of the Adversarial System of Government lets have a look at the institutions that exist within it but are not an actual part of the system. They are all operating within the paradigm but they are not producing it. It is however important to understand the entirety of our culture if we are looking to improve it. So what is the financial system when we try to look at the whole thing? This first piece of this puzzle is the foundation of the financial system. That foundation is so called free market capitalism. When you think of a free market you might envision an open market where anybody can go and sell anything they want. This is true, yet an actual physical market like a flea market or a mall or a convenience store actually sells tangible objects that you can see and touch and use.

But the financial market is so much more in comparison to history. In the beginning of civilization people simply bartered or traded with each other to fulfill their survival needs. Then came money. So money is just an object from a metal coin to a paper currency. The only value it has is the value that the system of government gives it. We all must participate in this financial paradigm. Back in the Roman Empire they had money with the inscription of Caesar on it. In the Bible Jesus asks the question of the coin, "whose inscription is on it"? They answered Caesar. The Jesus said "give unto Caesar what is Caesars and give unto God what is God's". But in this age we have a global financial system that transcends a single form of currency. We have a massive stock market and we have global stock markets that include everything. They sell Publicly owned companies in the form of stocks. You can buy everything from cattle futures to orange juice and soybean futures. You can buy gold you can buy the dollar you can buy options contracts called calls and puts. These are sold in the derivatives market.These are essentially contracts that you buy which gives you the right to buy a stock in the future. Calls are UP and Puts are Down.

This derivatives market in the world is estimated to be valued at 542 Trillion Dollars in open stock contracts (62). I find all of this to be incredible. I not certain that the entire planet has 542 trillion dollars in print. This massive system of finance is like a roaring machine in the background that never stops. You can almost hear it. So why does this matter? It matters because it can and has crashed multiple times throughout history. The so called great recession that happened in 2008 was nearly a great depression. Our government stopped it by bailing out the big banks and stimulating the financial system to prevent a great depression (63). All of this happened because people took out massive amounts of mortgages that had variable interest rates designed to jack up the interest rates by the banks so they could make a lot more money from people. In other words, greedy deceptive and dishonest tactics were employed by the banking system and we all ended up paying for it when it reached its breaking point (63).

So in essence the banks used lies and manipulation to sell people corrupted mortgages. And as a result it caused a ripple effect that crashed the entire market. So who authorized the banks to banks to sell these corrupt variable rates mortgages? The congress and Barney Frank in particular authorized this under the idea that the poor needed better access to lending. So in effect a person or couple making 50 thousand a year could get a $250,000 mortgage and the banks were all to happy to hand these out like candy on Halloween (63). Did the Government take responsibility for this massively poor judgement? Not at all. They adjusted their deceptive rhetoric to simply blame the banks and wall street in general.

The term Wall Street versus Main Street was born. The people of course went along with this and they started to hate Wall Street. The government conducting the bailouts of the banks and companies like General Motors were seen as the saviors of the people. They saved us from the Great Depression 2.0. President Obama told Bankers in a scolding manor. He said, "listen, I'm the only thing between you and the people with the pitchforks"(64). So again we see the full truth consumed in the fog of manipulative rhetoric. I don't claim to be an expert in finance. But as far as I can tell the global financial market is nothing more than a giant casino that we are all to some degree enslaved by. Right now the market under Donald Trump is seeing all time highs. So the economy is seen as being very good and very strong.

People see their Individual Retirement Accounts that are full of stocks and bonds right now and they have much more money. But as we all know this can't go on forever. At some point the market will crash again and like any market it will swing back and forth. We the people have absolutely no control over this. So with all of this invisible monopoly money traveling through the internet in online and even machine driven trades, what can be done? In all honesty I'm not sure. It is sort of like pandora's box has already been opened. If we just pulled the plug on the system the entire planet might plunge into financial chaos. Perhaps someday in the future a better way may be created and phased in over time.

So what are the positives of the system of free market capitalism? The common saying, 'The American Dream', has been commonplace for generations. What is the 'American Dream'. I think we actually have two definitions of this dream. The first definition is meant to simply look at the fact that we are a free country. People from all over the world want to come here and get a good job and live in a free society that is civilized and safe. This is especially true when the immigrant comes from a third world country. So if you live in Juarez Mexico, you see the direct activities of the drug cartels. These cartels are nothing short of terrorists of the criminal drug empire (65). Unlike Islamic terrorists, these terrorists are all about making money. Anybody who is seen as an unloyal person or informant or any other threat will be killed in a horrible way. They hang bodies from bridges, place heads on bridges. They will engage in any kind of atrocity they can think of to keep the people, the police and the politicians in line. This is a literal duplication of what we see ISIS and other terrorist organizations conducting on a regular basis.

So in these cases the American Dream is an effort to escape a life of poverty, life threats and general terror. They can claim asylum at the nearest port of entry. I won't get into the border crisis because it is not relevant to this discussion. The other version of the American Dream is to start a company and become independently wealthy. People dream of becoming millionaires and in some cases billionaires. If one looks at our history we see that the vast majority of huge advancements have come from this free market system. We see everything from the light bulb, the automobile, the computer and microchip, the television, the smartphone and the internet. So why did everything come from here in the United States? The reason is the free market system of capitalism and the American dream being realized by people who simply wanted to become rich. What evidence of this can we look at? The Population of the United States is around 330 million people. The population of China is around 1.4 Billion people. So just looking at the math one would think that most of the worlds innovations would come out of China. However, if we look at China in the present day they are not a free market capital system. The Chinese system is a sort of hybrid mix of absolute government control and massive manufacturing and sales to countries around the world. So what are they producing? They are producing everything we invent. They also like to steal what we create in both commercial products and military technology (66). So what is the main point here?

We need the free market capitalist system to remain in order to continue to be the world's greatest country or super power. The ambition of China is to overtake us as the world's greatest super power (67). They honestly can not do this because they are not innovating anything like we are constantly doing at least on the corporate level. China has massive factories and companies like Samsung that make our cell phones and televisions. They make just about everything and they sell it all to the world, especially us. So when I see President Trump going after China on things like fair trade I love it. China does everything it can to cheat the system. They manipulate the value of their own currency and they steal our intellectual property. So in essence China is a brutal dictatorship and is simultaneously engaging in this sort of corrupt system of capitalism. They made the entire country one gigantic factory with cities that are so massive they are unbelievable in scale (68).

Yet if you live in China and try to practice any form of religion you can join the millions of people currently residing in 're-education camps' (69). I want to share a story about China that a man told me many years agon this is unverified but I believed him. This man travelled to China on business trips on a regular basis. He told me that he heard a story about a man who had a little bit too much to drink in a bar or restaurant. The Chinese man began complaining about the Chinese government and the treatment of the people. Eventually the word got out to the Chinese Military Police that this man spoke out against the Government. Now this Chinese man had a wife and children. The government police located this man. They then took him and his entire family and changed each of their names. Each member of the family was taken to other families across the vast country of China. They were forced to become members of these other families. Problem solved. This is the current paradigm in the Chinese government and the lives of the Chinese people. The people are so oppressed in China that it is obvious that they are not going to become innovators. So China is like a parasite in this way. We create it, they steal it, they make it and sell it. So in comparing the USA and China, the value of the free market capitalism system becomes obvious.

However, under the current paradigm of free market capitalism under the adversarial paradigm there are problems and stark contradictions. The treatment of our people trying to live out the so called American Dream needs a closer look. We live in a time when an NFL quarterback can get a contract for over one hundred million dollars (70). The other members of the Pro football team also make millions of dollars based on their talent and position. Yet a Police Officer makes fifty or sixty thousand dollars a year in the best paying States. So one job is to advance a football down a field in a sport. The Police Job is to go out and risk your life everyday in real incidents some of which involve the use of deadly force. The NFL doesn't use deadly force, so how can this even be considered sane? From this point of view it is insane. But in free market capitalism this is a side effect of the systems paradigms. The NFL makes so much money that they can afford to pay athletes huge amounts of money. The football players all have agents and these agents negotiate these contracts on behalf of their clients, the athletes. Do these players have amazing athletic abilities? Yes they do. But is it right that they get paid a hundred million dollars for being an expert in throwing a football or catching the football or blocking people?

So what is the reason for this? The Police Officer is in effect a drain on the system. He or she is paid either by the town or the State in the case of the State Police. As a result, local and State governments will do anything they can to pay these Public Servants as little as they can get away with. The fact that their job might result in their death every day is irrelevant. This is all part of the system in free market capitalism. This paradigm is what politicians call 'income inequality' (71). Yet income inequality in the eyes of politicians look more at equal pay for women and minorities. This is not a bad thing, yet the huge inequality I just pointed out between the Police and the NFL is not even spoken of by politicians. Baseball and Basketball stars (as they are called) also receive massive compensation. The NFL has become a game of new rules that protect the quarterback in a huge way. We now have the concussion protocol for the players and if you touch the head of the quarterback it's a penalty. Are they doing this because they care about these players general welfare? Probably not for the most part. They are protecting a hundred million dollar asset in my opinion. Now the game becomes more and more boring and the fans are generally losing interest. Yet in boxing and MMA you hear nothing about any sort of concussion protection. Why is this? It is because the very nature of boxing or MMA is dependant on a concussive knockout. You can't remove the concussive knockout from MMA or Boxing if you want the sport to survive. So it's simply accepted as the paradigm.

We also see this in hollywood. A movie star is paid millions of dollars to act out a role. If you have the looks and the talent your agent will get you millions of dollars. This is because movies make so much money that movie studio companies can afford to pay this much and still make huge amounts of money. These so called movie stars are glorified as the rich and famous and they actually have a larger voice than the rest of us regarding politics. People will listen to these actors and place extended value on their opinions only because they are rich and famous. So we are in essence listening to Hollywood rhetoric. NFL Stars are so called role models, we look up to them and place extended value on their opinions. Take Colin Kaepernick, the quarterback as an example. He decided to 'take a knee' during the national anthem as a form of protest and created a huge scandal that was all over the national news media (72). Most people weighed in and took their perspective sides on the issues that this athlete expressed. This role model was taken very seriously and politicians even weighed in on it.

The idea of 'a living wage' is talked about by politicians like Bernie Sanders (self proclaimed socialist). One side wants socialism to replace free market capitalism and the other side calls this notion madness that will destroy the very fabric of our financial super power. When you break down the idea of socialism, it's simply the idea of the government taking peoples money away. Then the government gives it back to the people in the proportions that they consider just and right for everyone. As I previously mentioned, socialism has failed in every country it has been adopted in. So we have capitalism and socialism as our only two options(54).

Why are these two options the only options available. Well, as I mentioned earlier, we are lacking in the areas of original thought and visionaries like our founding fathers. On one hand we have the need for competition, free market capitalism and the American dream. On the other hand we have people scraping a living and not earning a living wage. In the past families only needed one breadwinner and the mother could stay home and raise the children (if she chose to do so). In the present, most couples both have to work in order to survive financially. So how do we get people a living wage while maintaining free market capitalism, competition and the dream of making a billion dollars by owning a company?

As I mentioned, this silly idea of socialism (54) is the government taking peoples money and then giving back in the form of wealth redistribution will destroy our financial system and the American dream. So when you look at the NFL they pay out these huge sums of money to the athletes based on the vast money the NFL makes. So what about huge corporations worth hundreds of billions of dollars? What do they do with the vast wealth they accumulate? We now have the highest levels in the stock market in the history of our country. One would think that these companies would be paying their employees more money. The sad truth is that these Public companies have CEOs and what they call shareholders or the corporate board. According to the media most of these companies are taking these profits and using to do what they call stock buybacks. So the market is up 50 percent and massive companies use the money to buy their own stock. Yet we can't stop this or we will be a socialist country. So what is option three?

One thing we can do is create a win win situation. When I was in a management position I always looked at the opportunity for a win win as a great solution in the art of problem solving. So instead of passing a law to create socialism in America we can pass a law that gives money to the people and not to the government to give it to the people. So what would this law look like? We need to keep capitalism alive and competition alive to remain the superpower we are. The law in my opinion would be called something like 'The Fair Compensation Act'. This would be fair for the company and the employees of the company. So we take a percentage of the companies profit and make it a law that it is passed on to the employees. Let's say the percentage is 7 percent or even 10 percent. This leaves 90 percent of the profit in the hands of the rich people at the top of the company.

I was watching President Trump on TV a few days ago. He was at an Apple plant in Texas with the CEO of Apple Tim Cook. The President said that Apple was worth 1.3 Trillion dollars(73). Do you think that apple will do the same thing as the NFL and pay the employees a salary proportionate to the amount of money they make? Not in a million years. If the employees of Apple in the United States made ten percent of the companies profit they would effectively be fairly rich or well off. So as a consequence a job at Apple would be highly sought after and create competition in the workplace. Yet Apple's shareholders and board of Directors would still remain the super rich since they have access to 90 percent of the prophet.

Like the founding fathers we need to look at every way this can be corrupted and assure that it is not. So what about companies that are not on the stock exchange? Well they have to do the same thing with their money. What about small businesses and startups? For new or small businesses a certain level of wealth would have to be obtained by the owner before this law applies. So a number must be set to establish what net worth of the owner must be before this law comes into play. It should be the standard of a rich man. That standard is generally considered to be 'set for life as they say'. So let's say 3 million dollars. So after the business owner or CEO is at a net worth of 3 million he or she must apply the fair compensation act. Then what if the owner hides the money offshore or places it in some kind of trust fund or other type of account. Well that would become illegal fraud.

What about the idea we always hear about that says 'if we do this, the cost will simply be made up for by charging the consumer more'. Well that would be illegal profiteering. What if the companies simply leave the United States and do business in China or Vietnam? This is an important one. We need to only allow a certain percentage of a business to operate overseas. This is a matter of national security. If we find ourselves in a major war we need the majority of manufacturing to be right here in the United States. This also prevent companies from getting around fair compensation act. The profits made by a company that is American overseas will also be included the fair compensation act for American employees. So how would this affect the economy? One thing will be a modest drop in the value of the stock or private company. With profiteering being illegal, people will have more money to buy the same things at the same price. What about the people in the hierarchy of the company? Do they just get paid the same from top to bottom? No, the employee gets a normal base pay depending on the job, so a janitor will still not make the same money as the supervisors and scientist and plant managers and so forth. The fair compensation act is money above and beyond the actual base salary. So it will actually fluctuate with the market value of the company or stock. This would actually inspire people to do a good job, be innovative, save money and increase the value of the company. These goals in the present are only worried about by the big bosses CEO's and shareholders.

Will this law guarantee that every American gets a huge increase in income? No but I think it's the best way to help as many people as possible and preserve the free market capital system. So is this just socialism 2.0? No it isn't, this is a system of pure competition. The highest paid people will be working for the most successful companies. This means that the best companies will attract the best people. The worst companies will not attract the best people. So the law of the capitalistic jungle are still in full effect. But the philosophy is simple. Give the money to the people not the government. I heard the founder of Microsoft Bill Gates on TV recently said that he paid ten billion dollars in taxes. He said he would be willing to pay 20 billion but 100 billion would be a bit much (74). Many of these mega billionaires want to see this country prosper and are leaning towards socialism themselves as an option. The notion of not allowing companies to raise prices beyond a certain level is already in effect. The Chairman of the Federal Reserve currently adjusts interest rates to control both inflation and deflation (77). If this is allowed, the crime of profiteering preventing companies from just charging more is just and fair.

So what will the government want to do in this new paradigm of the fair compensation act? Like they always do, they will be salivating at this grand opportunity to raise your taxes. This will also be illegal on both the State and Federal level under the fair compensation act. So what will be the positive effects of this new law? This would very effectively stimulate the economy. People will have more money and they will as a consequence purchase more and better products. So a person who used to only be able to buy a used car will buy a new car.

People will buy bigger houses and bigger televisions and more expensive phones and computers and every other product in existence.

As a consequence of this people will be paying more State and Federal taxes along with property and car taxes. All this does is take money that is parked on the stock market or non public companies coffers and puts it into circulation. The companies that make products will sell more of the best products and will be making more money and paying more taxes. So the value of the company will rise and the rich get richer and the employees make more money. So the cycle goes on and on. With the government making more money in taxes they will be able to double the pay of our military members. This is a just cause for obvious reasons. These soldiers, sailors and airmen and marines deserve a good living since they, even more than the Police risk their lives and die on the field of battle.

Another benefit is the remaining law of the capitalist jungle will make it very difficult for what I call shady businesses. So if you run one of these small used car dealerships that are selling pieces of junk for exorbitant prices your basically screwed. People can't make much money working for you. So you will have to either change your business model to a high class operation and perhaps form a franchise or you can go out of business. But the main point is that law will increase competition. So with the used car example you will see higher standards and perhaps more competitive used car franchises form. So in looking at this whole idea it's another advancement in civilization that both cares for and motivates the people and businesses to improve in every way.

One negative I see is the consequence to States who do not have any form of State income tax. Nine States in the country do not have an income tax (75). These States will probably need to impose the taxes in order to pay a fair wage in order to pay and attract Public Servants of every type. Yet the people in these States will be making more money and it will not break them. However the States just like the government will not be allowed to charge massive taxes. They will make more money in taxes anyway and only a reasonable tax in the present day will be allowed to be imposed to both people and businesses.

So how will this help Public Servants who rely on the Town, State or Federal Government? It honestly won't help them as much. But with the population earning so much more money the amount of taxes will increase. So we should in theory be able to pay Public Servants twice what they are paid now. Nothing will fix everything, but the idea of a living wage can be done by business, it can't be done by Socialism. Even Bernie Sanders with his fifteen dollar an hour minimum wage promise won't solve the problem (76). In this time, that amount of money is not a living wage if we are honest. Besides Mcdonalds and Burger King sharing 10 percent of profits with the employees would become quite a decent living. And by law they can't charge 20 dollars for a big mack. So this is the best win win I can envision in the financial system we are in under the current paradigms.

CHAPTER 15
'The United States Military'

The United States has the most powerful military in the history of the world. This is a fairly well known fact. So if we establish a new paradigm that is a non adversarial system of government, do we still need the most powerful military is history? In all reality I think we need an even more powerful military. Just because we have an advanced civilization, that does not at all mean that the rest of the world is civilized at all. If we change to a non adversarial paradigm I predict that the other Democracies in Europe and other places will follow suit. This doesn't include countries like Russia, China, North Korea and Iran.

In fact I would submit to you the opinion that in the eyes of countries like Russia and China they view us and our system as pure weakness. We don't get done what a dictator can get done and all we do is argue and stagnate in this pathetic democratic system of weakness and lack of leadership. One piece of evidence that illustrates the view that Russia has of us, is this so called 'election interference' (78). Russia places large numbers of social media messages up to spread propaganda that will influence the American people to vote for the candidate they desire. The Russians also feel that they can literally disrupt our country by spreading divisive propaganda to turn us against each other and create chaos all over our country. If we are that gullible, that we could buy into this sort of propaganda then the systemic changes I'm suggesting are all the more necessary. Our political leaders in my view believe that we are that stupid and that easily influenced. They are the only ones allowed to influence us. To politicians this Russia spam is a threat to their influence over you and they consider it an act of war to some degree. I personally can see right through any influence, rhetoric or propaganda. If you can't, you can expand your own thinking and avoid all of this nonsense being thrown at you. Moving on to a true military level, what do we have to protect us from being invaded and ruled over?

In the present moment China has a little over two million troops (79). If China went into full boar draft mode I would imagine that hundreds of million troops or more could be achieved (79). The United States currently has 1.3 million active troops and 865 thousand in reserve (80). In a full blown world war draft we could amass around 70 million or more (80). If we are talking about Russia or China invading us they would have to cross an ocean to do it. I would imagine that they would never make it here to begin with, they would be destroyed at sea even if we had to nuke the Ocean. Our technology is far superior to both of these enemies. They are working hard to catch up and China has a bad habit of stealing our military technology through espionage or even hacking. China in all truth is more interested in making money than they are defeating us in war. They want to replace us as the world's largest superpower (67). Vladimir Putin wants to invade Europe and establish a second Soviet Union (81). Yet they know better in my view. So we see them taking small steps like the invasion of Ukraine. They took a small portion including a port of strategic significance. We, as you see in the media give the Ukrainians military hardware to fight the Russians and keep them from invading the entire country. So is Russia a threat? Yes, in my opinion, but they are also realists, they know that at the end of the day they will lose to both Europe and the United States. If Russia were to join forces with China I feel that would be difficult but even then one way or another we will win. We have proven this in two world wars.

The odds are in my opinion that we won't have to fight either Russia or China. In terms of actual threats we must examine the lunatics in the world. Many people say that North Korea and their nuclear arsenal are a legitimate threat. We still have 23 thousand troops in South Korea right on the border of North Korea (82). The Korean war has never actually ended (83). We consider Kim Jong Un the North Korean dictator to be a lunatic of sorts in my view. He likes to be provocative and do missile tests and test nuclear weapons from time to time (84). In my opinion Mr. Un realizes that the minute he attacks South Korea he's committing suicide. If he uses a nuclear weapon he knows that just two of our nuclear submarines could erase his entire country in about 20 minutes. So yes Kim Jong UN is a monster and a killer who treats his people like nothing less than non human objects. Night time satellite photos of North Korea show that at least half of the country has no electrical power (85). People are starving in North Korea and they are cut off from the outside world (86). Most North Koreans believe that the United States is simply out to kill them all and that we are the most vicious enemy in the world (87).

This propaganda is just one of the ways Kim Jong Un controls his people (87). Does this mean he is stupid enough to go to war with us either conventionally or on a nuclear level? No he isn't in my view, and the fact that he has not done anything beyond weapons testing and military exercises is evidence of this. It could happen but in my opinion it is unlikely. The Chinese also have a leash on him in my opinion. They want to make money off of us and they will likely not allow Mr. Un to attack us or

South Korea. If the Chinese saw that threat is imminent they just might take over North Korea themselves. China is a miserable country to live in, yet in comparison to North Korea living under Chinese rule would we be wonderful to the people in North Korea. They would actually have electricity and food.

So what country is the biggest lunatic? That would be Iran. Iran is under a religious need to actually start a world war. The so called Mahdi (88) is a sort of Messiah figure in the Iranian World of Islam. The Mahdi in their opinion existed in the ninth century and then disappeared from humanity. The Mahdi can only return in the midst of a massive world war type of calamity. Many people have observed Iran in the media shooting down our drones and attacking a Saudi Arabian oil refinery and attacking or even stealing other countries oil tankers (89). People are puzzled by this in my opinion. They ask why would Iran do this? What is Iran's motive to escalate things, it makes no tactical sense, they can't win? Even other Islamic States likely can't understand why Iran is doing what it is doing. Well the reason they are doing all of this is because they actually want to start a world war in my view. This will create the required environment of chaos and war that will usher in the return of the Mahdi. This Mahdi will then bring world peace (88). So this lunacy actually exists in the twenty first century. With regard to Israel, Iran wants to, in their own words, "wipe them off the map" (90).

So given all of this so called religious motivation to start a world war, what happens when they succeed in creating nuclear weapons? Will they actually launch a nuclear attack on Israel? We can't say they will with total certainty. It really comes down to religious fervor and the suicidal nature of the attack. In other words, will they have the courage of their religious convictions? Although we can't say they will for sure, we can say another thing for sure. Israel will be in a position in which they can't afford but to assume they will. In that scenario Israel may in fact conduct a nuclear strike in Iran or bomb and invade Iran outright without nuclear weapons. This conflict could quickly escalate if other Islamic nations attack Israel in the region. We are allies to Israel (91) and Russia is allied with Iran (92). That's a scenario that has worried the world for a long time. Some Christians see this as an Armageddon scenario that may usher in the second coming of Christ (93). How Ironic, Iran wants to usher in a Mahdi to create a peaceful world by starting Armageddon to usher in the second coming of Christ according to the Christian faith.

Regardless of what you believe, Iran is a lunatic country with a lunatic belief system and are conducting acts of lunacy and attacking a large variety of different countries in different ways. They attacked a Japanese oil tanker (94), and the list is growing and will continue to grow. If we know this is inevitable what if anything should we do about it? President Trump ended the Iran Nuclear Deal as it was called (95). Iran is suffering on an economic level which has been seen as part of the reason for Iran's sudden aggression streak (96). Then again they want chaos and global war anyway. So yes, we poked the lunatic and maybe that can be a cause of their behavior, but it can't be the only reason given the religious war goal they have. I personally realize that like most of us that I don't have all of the information. I'm pretty sure we have contingency plans in place that involve both the United States and Israel. In the first Gulf war Saddam Hussein launched cheap Russian Scud missiles at Israel in an attempt to escalate the war into a regional conflict. Israel ignored these attacks and we provided them with Patriot anti missile defence systems. Since then we have created the so called Iron Dome in Israel which is used to protect Israel from missile attacks from Hamas. This is also in place to protect them from Iran (97).

I realize that Americans are war weary at this point. However if this Iran problem comes down to a situation of fight me now and many less people die than fight me later it's kind of obvious. We may in fact need to get this over with before Iran tries to conduct a nuclear attack on Israel. At this point in the eventual progression of things we would need to destroy Iran's entire nuclear program and it's military assets in my view. If we wait until Iran forces Israel to attack we may be walking into a regional war that could escalate into a much larger conflict. Iran's nuclear program is located in bunkers so deep that a bunker buster bomb wont even come close to penetrating it (98). Some people have talked about using some kind of nuclear bunker buster if there is such a thing. More than likely I think we will need to go in there on the ground and take these sites out. Nothing is impenetrable on the ground. I don't think President Trump will do this in his first term. If he gets elected to a second term he may need to do this. Again it is important to stress that I don't have all of the information that the military and intelligence communities have. Maybe there is a third option that none of us know about. I hope this is the case because I am genuinely tired of war like most people. However if we do end up doing this I will fully support it as a wise decision. Imagine if we just invaded Germany before Hitler took over Europe. Would that have been a good call, and did we see it coming for a long time before we got involved? We can never learn too much from history in my opinion.

How does this problem fit into our current politics and so called political correctness? If I'm observing this apocalyptic version of Islam in a negative way, I could be considered Islamophobic (99) or Xenophobic (the fear of people from other countries) (100). So am I suffering from a phobia of Islam? Is this like people who are afraid of heights or am I suffering from the Islamic version of Arachnophobia, the fear and terror of spiders? The answer is no. What we are dealing with here is an apocalyptic version of Islam seeking to start a world war. Yet there is a distinct difference in this religion. The religion itself is the government, and the government is controlling the Iranian military. The Iranian military is blowing up Saudi oil refineries and highjacking oil carrying super tankers owned by other countries. So in this case I suppose you could label me as being Iran concerned. Anybody who is observing this problem with Iran would be justified in feeling concerned or even afraid in some cases. When your religion becomes a government with a military you become more than a religion, you become a nation. Nations are subject to international law, other nations have the right to defend themselves against any other nation. So liberals or others should not label this in any way. Iran is a problem and the politicians all agree on this in my opinion.

If it were up to me, I would boil this down to the root problem which is this apocalyptic version of Islam. I would bomb the Ayatollahs residence with 20 thousand pound MOAB bomb and take out all of the religious leaders pushing this nonsense. Then I would send in the 82nd Airborne Division along with a large contingency of Army Rangers to take out the nuclear program. Simultaneously I would bomb the entire Iranian Military, especially their Iranian Republican Guard. After the nuclear program is gone along with the Iranian military divisions we would leave. Then we would use our intelligence community to incite an uprising of the people causing a regime change. I don't think this would be politically correct and accepted.

But then again war is not politically correct. The people of Iran are already trying to rise up and protest the impoverished state of their lives (101). The people are suffering and want change. Should we make some attempt to prevent an Islamic Republic?

No, because it will happen at some point regardless of anything we do as a consequence of the system of government attached to the Islamic Religion. What we need is a moderate Islamic Republic (if there is such a thing). We need something like the system in Dubai or Kuwait. These Islamic Republics encourage big business with the west. With Iran floating on a sea of oil they could prosper and become a nation of big business and by proxy become a non threat to the rest of the middle east and Especially Israel.

Regarding the pay of the service members in our military, as I mentioned in the previous chapter on the financial system, they should get double their current pay. The concept of a fair compensation act will make this possible. We have an all volunteer military (102). So to encourage recruitment in my opinion we should maintain a twenty year and out system with a full pay retirement and full medical benefits for life. This should bring in just the kind of Patriots we are looking for and make the job attractive to people. The military should never be seen by our leaders as a financial drain on the system. They should be viewed as highly regarded protectors of our freedom in our homeland. Advanced next level weapon systems should continue to evolve and in my opinion we should increase the size of the military by at least 25 percent. This will allow us to be able to fight wars on multiple fronts if necessary. If you the reader are not educated on the weapons systems we have developed. I would advise you to watch some youtube videos on things like the 'sensor fuzed munition' (103). Our M1-Abrahms tank can hit targets from two miles out while our enemies have a tank range of one mile (104). These and other systems like the F22 Raptor fighter bomber are miles ahead of our potential enemies (105). This needs to continue on and on until the world no longer has any wars at all.

One paradigm in weapons systems I have questioned for years is the simple concept of the bullet. A bullet has the tip which is the actual projectile, it has a case that holds the gun powder, and finally, it has a primer that ignites the gunpowder which explodes the gunpowder sending the bullet down range. Our current weapon of war is a .223 caliber bullet. This is a small caliber bullet weight that travels at high velocities, it basically a glorified .22 caliber round. In the past we had the M1-Garand rifle which employed a 30 caliber round (106). It held less bullets yet it had far superior stopping power. This of course was a heavier bullet and less rounds could be carried by the soldiers. What if you replaced gunpowder with a very small amount of high explosive to explode the bullet down range just like gunpowder does? What would the advantage be with this? You would have a high power round like a .308 or 30-06 round that is an inch in length or a bit more.

This would allow a soldier to carry 600 rounds or more and use 150 round magazines of high power rifle rounds. If we can make a 'sensor fuze munition', I'm sure we can create a long overdue upgrade of the common bullet which hasn't changed in over 100 years. Perhaps this would be too expensive. Then again this expense would help us win wars and create a firestorm capacity for our soldiers on the field of battle. These new bullets can be applied to everything from the military rifle, to the 50 caliber machine guns, to the sniper rifle and all the way up to the huge 30 millimeter gun used in the A-10 Warthog aircraft (107). Think of an A-10 Warthog that can carry five times the number of rounds it currently holds, could be seen as useful to the military? Of course it would. Perhaps high explosive propellant will foul the weapon and cause jams. I don't know, but I do know that we could create a clean burning explosive in the military round if a proper explosive does not currently exist. Or you could even try to develop a super concentrated high power new gunpowder as an option. The idea is a far smaller and more powerful bullet. Current gun powder fouls a weapon to the point that it needs to be cleaned by the soldier every time it is used on the field of battle. This is just a thought for people in the world of weapons design and manufacturing. And of course these bullets should not be available to the general public.

CHAPTER 16
'The Intelligence Community'

The world of the intelligence community is a controversial subject in this day and age. In the post nine eleven world we have a total of seventeen intelligence agencies that work separately and together (108). They do everything from espionage to listening in on people's phone calls and tracking terrorists all over the world. Edward Snowden is considered a traitor by the government for releasing hundreds of thousands of top secret documents outlining a large number of Government programs (109). He revealed that we are being watched by the National Security Agency (NSA) (109). So this created questions about our right to privacy and people took sides on the issue like all other issues (110). Some people hated the idea and felt fearful or paranoid about being listened to and watched by the government. Conspiracy theorists had a field day with this saying, "see I told you this was happening", "none of us are safe from big brother"(110). So in the post nine eleven world everything has changed ranging from the Intelligence Community to Law Enforcement. We have the Patriot Act (111) in effect and a terrorist detainment camp in Cuba's Guantanamo Bay (112). All of this happened as a result of nine eleven (113). Now when we go to the airport it's like going through a series of walls that make us safe in the form of mandatory security measures.

Why are all of these changes needed? Is this just the government taking advantage of a crisis with the goal of gradually stripping us of our freedoms? These are fair questions that the people are allowed to ask. To examine all of this we need to look at what information we do have in the world of the intelligence community. Information on these agencies is very limited since these agencies are all top secret. One thing we can look at is a quote by former President Barack Obama. The President said, "I continue to be much more concerned, when it comes to our security, with the prospect of a nuclear weapon going off in Manhattan" (114). What does this tell us? It's simple and obvious in my view, the end game ambition of terrorists is an eventual nuclear attack in New York City or some other major city. Don't we already know this on a common sense level?

What would happen if terrorists managed to destroy an entire American city. I can only take a guess on this scenario. I personally think that once people in every major American city hear that another city has been utterly destroyed by a nuclear weapon terrorist attack the reaction will be huge. People in every major population center will want to quickly get out of the city immediately. This will cause multiple mass exodus problems ranging from unbelievable traffic jams to the suburbs being consumed by millions of people. Grocery stores and gas stations in the path of this exodus will run out of both food and fuel. People will then get hungry and run out of gas. Then we will see tribal behavior emerge with some people doing whatever they have to do to feed themselves and their children. All of these fleeing masses would not be going to work which will tank the stock market. I'm sure this is only a sample of the chaos that would ensue in a nuclear terrorist attack. So what would the government be forced to do in such a scenario? Martial law I believe, would need to be enacted immediately after the attack to force people to remain in the cities and go to work and continue with their normal lives. This means that the military would take control of the population and maintain order to prevent the country and the economy from falling into a state of chaos. This is a scenario that we must prevent from ever happening.

Who are the people in the best position to prevent this from ever happening? That would be the intelligence community. How would they ever pick up on this information before the attack comes to fruition? They would need every type of intel they can get their hands on and detect the efforts of terrorists seeking to either obtain or build an atomic weapon. We must prevent it from reaching our shores. So perhaps this helps to explain the need to listen to 'everything'. I heard a rumor years ago (unverified) that the government has football stadium sized underground sites with massive numbers of computers listening to everyone in the world. I heard (in this rumor) that they picked up on keywords that would automatically trigger an alert and record the conversation and identify the persons talking and also locate them. Is this true? I have no idea, but it's possible.

In the present day everything from phones to text messages to social media would need to be monitored. Yet if this is happening how do things like the Boston Marathon bombing happen (115)? Like every system, whatever they are, they are not perfect. When nine eleven happened I was still working in my career and we all had absolutely no reason to assume that the 911 attack was over. We had to assume that the World Trade Center and Pentagon attack were only the beginning. We discussed the potential of hundreds of terrorists being already in country and preparing to attack.

Another piece of information worth looking at is the simple fact that we have not had 25 or more major terrorist attacks after 911. The bounty on Al-Baghdadi the founder of the ISIS caliphate was 25 million dollars (116). We know from listening to President Trump that we had an inside source in the compound when he was killed in by our special forces (117). I would assume that this inside source left with their family with the troops who killed Baghdadi. This source and their family are probably in Wyoming right now with 25 million dollars in the witness protection program with new identities. So we all know that money talks as they say. In my opinion we pay poor people a lot of money in terrorist hot spots to identify terrorist plotting attacks inside and outside of the United States. Once identified Navy Seals or other similar special forces units take these people out before they are even done planning. So between listening to everyone and intelligence operations on the ground we have prevented the 25 major terrorist attacks that would have each killed thousands of people in the United States. We never hear about it, but I must assume based on the very limited number of attacks inside of our country that these things are happening on a regular basis.

I'm sure that much more than what I've hypothesized is happening to keep us safe. Going back to the topic of the people's right to privacy, it's complicated. Some advocates of privacy rights may respond to my writing here by saying 'hey pal those attacks are the price of freedom'. If you the reader feel that way I respect your opinion. Personally, with the ever evolving state of technological advancement in the world it's all worth it. Why? It is simply going to become easier and easier to construct a nuclear weapon in a third world country and transport it here. Losing millions of Americans can be the price of freedom and privacy, or losing some of our privacy is the price of living. You can decide these options on your own as a free person. But one thing that is good to remember is that if your living a normal crime free life. The intelligence community likely doesn't want to waste valuable time and resources spying on your phone calls with your friends and family.

With regard to all of the things that are considered top secret by the Government and the Military. People may not agree with me on this, but this needs to continue. Things are top secret for a reason in my view. So to give an example, let's go into movie mode for a minute. Suppose that government scientists working for the military actually discovered a new and incredible power source capable of providing free green electricity for the entire planet. One might think, hey that is wonderful. Yet this energy source could be used as a weapon a thousand times more powerful than a nuclear warhead. Does this need to remain top secret? Of course it does unless we all want to die. That ends the sci fi movie mode. I think we have no choice but to assume things are top secret for a reason. If it is a corrupt reason like keeping the oil market alive with a safe energy source being concealed, that would be quite wrong. Sooner or later someone like Snowden the traitor (109) would leak it out.

CHAPTER 17

'Law Enforcement and Security'

I'm going to start by exploring the general treatment of our Police Officers by the population at large. If we examine the older generations we will (mostly) find that older people do not want to give the Police a hard or abusive time (unless provoked in some cases). In my generation you just knew better than to mess with the Police. They would ruin your day one way or another. I recall a saying from my youth. "You never win an argument with a cop or a school teacher". If you were actually stupid enough to put your hands on a cop, well you were going to regret that in any number of ways.

In looking at the younger so called millennial generation (118), it's as if they have been educated in how to make a cops job a living hell. In recent events in New York City we watched in amazement on the news as people just walked up to the police and doused them with water right in the face (119). The police actually just walked away to avoid getting into trouble. This would indicate that city and the Police Department did not have their backs on this non lethal assault of a Police Officer which is a felony. If people tried that 20 years ago they would have been sprayed with pepper spray and slammed on the ground before being handcuffed and arrested. Eventually after this water dousing began to increase a law was passed to allow the Police in NYPD to arrest anyone doing this to a Police Officer (119). But in this age of politics being anti police in the liberal parts of the country, the Police are treated as if they are enemies who are oppressing the poor and less fortunate. Yet when people need the Police they completely reverse this attitude and call 911 screaming for help of every variety in my experience.

Do the Police have a right to be respected? No they do not. Can they have their Peace Breached and charge you with Breach of Peace? No their peace can not be breached, that's part of the job. So how should we treat the men and women in the Law Enforcement Community? In my opinion we should at least start off by being respectful at a minimum. If you start off as a respectful compliant person and the officer treats you like trash. Then you can make a choice to push back verbally or just not bother reacting. You can always file a complaint at the Police Department later. Do some Police Officers have bad days and treat people like dirt, yes some do. Are some officers nasty to people all of the time as a regular practice? Yes a few are like that and they are in the wrong job for the most part.

If you need to push back verbally on a Police Officer you need to be careful of what comes out of your mouth. If you threaten a police officer or in anyway or interfere with his or her investigation you may be subject to arrest. So why are some Officers nicer than others? Well one obvious reason is that some cops are just not the best of people. Some are on a power trip and this is usually a newer younger cop who lacks experience. Not all, but many older experienced cops have learned to leave the ego at the door and least give people a chance to be respectful and treat them with common decency. In my experience, I've noticed that some officers hunt people and some officers serve people. Younger Officer tend to hunt more than older officers and they even view the older more measured officers as useless. But if we are to be really honest, we must acknowledge that some officers are in fact afraid. It's a real advantage to a civilian if they are able to see the world through the eyes of a Police Officer on duty.

Police officers are highly trained to survive everything that they may encounter on the job. This includes everything from traffic stops to domestic violence calls to active shooter scenarios. One must always remember that when they are stopped or interviewed by the Police that the Officer neither knows or trusts you. They watch a stranger's body language for signs of aggression and they want you to keep your hands out of your pockets. This includes both pants pockets and coat pockets. They may ask you to sit down on the curb or the steps. Why? Because you are less able to quickly attack them while you are seated. If you are 250 lb large male who has been drinking they may even handcuff you for officer safety. Many Police officers have stopped a vehicle and walked to the drivers window and were immediately shot and killed by the driver without warning.

The Police watch videos of these incidents from dash cams during their training. Every time they walk up to a vehicle they are in a sort of hyper state of awareness. They may even have their hand on their undrawn gun as they approach the vehicle. Regarding domestic violence calls, these calls are very dangerous and they generally use two officers to make contact. They are aware that people are highly agitated and emotional during bad arguments or fights. They may be armed or mentally ill or suicidal. So the first order of business is to establish their own safety in the incident. They will ask the arguing people if they have any weapons, if anybody has been assaulted. They will ask if there are any firearms on premisses. They may pat people down for weapons and handcuff them for safety. It all depends on the situation and mentality of the Police Officer.

There was a recent national case on Television where a female Police Officer walked into the wrong apartment in her apartment complex after work. So she sees a black male in what she believes is her home. She draws down on this guy with her gun and unfortunately she ends up shooting this man dead in his own house (120). I used to teach people about what was called fight or flight mode. This is a fight or flight style mechanism in the human brain. When your fear raises your heart rate to a very high level, your mind and body reacts. Most of your blood goes to your major organs including your brain and you get a sort of tunnel vision and the whole world feels like it slows down and you have a massive adrenaline dump (121).

The world around you appears to be moving more slowly. The reason for this slowdown of reality is the simple fact that your mind is running so fast that it creates this effect. Some of you may have experienced this at some dangerous point in your life. Some people fight and some people run. This female Officer who shot the man in his own apartment seems almost impossible from a regular logical persons point of view. You may ask how could this even happen? Did she not notice that the furniture and lamps and TV in the victim's house were not hers? How could she not see that she was in a different home? If I were a betting man I would bet that she saw this man in what she thought was her apartment and she went into survival mode based on her training. She was a new and young officer. She had such tunnel vision that all of the evidence that she was in the wrong home simply disappeared in her sea of adrenalin and survival mode. She thought she was going to die at the hands of a home invader and she shot this man in what she believed was self defense.

This tragedy was an awful thing and I feel terrible for this poor man who died needlessly. I also feel bad for the Officer who was convicted of Murder. So how does one prevent this survival mode in a civilian or military or police situation. Breathing deeply can help a little, but one must simply learn how to not allow that initial first reaction of panic and control one's own fear. Some of this comes naturally to some and others can learn this through experience. A seasoned excellent cop or soldier or civilian can literally walk into a life threatening situation without there heart rate raising at all. They also learn that when they run in pursuit they tend to get an adrenal spike. They also realize that when they are in a high speed vehicle chase that it will spike their adrenalin. I'm sure most of you have watched some TV shows like Cops (122) and watched a high speed chase. One thing you will usually see is the Officer on the radio speaking as calmly as possible as he or she calls in the ever changing direction of travel of the suspect vehicle. Eventually the criminals car stops and you almost always see the same ending. A bunch of cops run up to the suspects vehicle screaming "get on the ground, get on the ground" at the top of their lungs. They then rip the suspect out of the car door or window and slam him or her to the ground. They are usually all adrenalized by the time the pursuit ends. This is a sort of evidence of my point about Police survival instinct and the power of fear and adrenaline.

Every time I was involved in a foot chase with my officers and it ended with the suspect on the ground and handcuffed I did one thing. I would assess the mindset of my people and look for signs of survival mode adrenalin. If I saw an officer who looked like he or she was about loose it and kick this person or something, I would very calmly say to them, it's over take five. They would usually take a deep breath and walk away to calm down. People in uniform are people and they make mistakes just like everyone else. So to anybody reading this I would advise you to be aware of the potential effects of an adrenalized person be it an officer or some angry guy in a convenience store losing their mind.

I am obviously a person who supports law enforcement and security personnel. I do however want to share with you some ways that you can put an officer at ease (somewhat) if you are pulled over or approached for an interview. So now we can sort of see things through the eyes of an officer. If you get pulled over at night, turn on your interior light so the officer can see the interior of the car as he checks it visually for weapons of drugs. Before the officer ever reaches your drivers or passenger side window open your glove compartment and leave it open. Retrieve your registration and insurance card along with your driver's license. Hold all three of these things in one hand (your left hand if on the cops approaching the drivers side). Then while holding these three items the cop will want, place both hands on the steering wheel and leave them there until the officer asks for them.

He or she will shine a light on you and look around your whole vehicle. Yet he or she will see you as a less likely threat scenario. Be calm and direct in your conversation and just answer the cops questions. If you have a gun on you with a legal carry permit just leave it in the holster and have your pistol permit in your hand and tell the officer that your armed. Hopefully the officer won't freak out but he or she will likely need to have you step out of the car so you can be disarmed. Be certain to not make any sudden rapid movements during the disarming. Always remember that cops are twitchy and as we saw in the Texas accidental muder an inexperienced cop may overreact. If the cop freaks out and spins you around and pushes you into the car to disarm you don't react in any way. If you are seen as resisting while armed by some rookie you may end up staring down his or her gun barrel. Again if you are mistreated you can always make a complaint afterwards.

Another scenario to understand is the reality in the mind of a SWAT unit. So let's assume an unlikely scenario. A swat team has accidentally gone to your home and thinks your a barricaded armed suspect with hostages. If they call the actual home of the Suspect to establish communication your not going to be able to answer the phone. So you and your family are sitting there watching TV and a bunch of tactical units smash open the door with a ram and are pointing rifles at your face screaming get on the floor over and over. It should be obvious that you should get on the floor and they will zip tie cuff you and start clearing the house room by room. If you're not too smart you might stand up and go off on the SWAT team for invading your space. You will either be taken down or tazed or even accidentally shot. So to make it simple, you must understand that the mind set of SWAT units are extreme. They will take control of everything in minutes depending on the building. And all they are thinking about is shoot or don't shoot along with saving lives from being lost to the worst criminals.

I think that understanding the thinking of Law Enforcement should be taught in schools so people can effectively communicate with them based on their priorities. Once you understand the fears and priorities of law enforcement you can behave and communicate in a way that will make the experience less negative or even dangerous to yourself.

Regarding Security Officers we must reveal the differences between the Police and Private Security Officers. Security officers have been harshly labeled in our culture. They get called fake cop, mall cop or rent a cops. Yet in my experience I have learned that in the post 911 world Security Officers have been retasked and pretty highly trained in many instances. Some are armed and some are not. Many times security forces are called Public Safety Officers. So in my experience I have learned that before 911 the primary job of a Security Officer was to only observe and report incidents. In other words, they were not allowed to do much of anything in managing incidents besides calling the Police. In the present Public Safety Officers from College Campuses to Malls and Hospitals have become full contact Security units. So the days of observe and report for the most part are over.

The Officers will use force just like the Police in violent incidents. They are trained in what is known as the force continuum. This is the simple concept of reacting to force against the Officer or victim with force one level up from the force being perpetrated. So if someone takes a swing at a Public Safety Officer they may pepper spray the subject, take him or her to the ground and apply handcuffs. This new world of security also applies to the most insulted security of all. Mall Security. Mall Security is often trained in the same way that cops are in self defence and pepper spray and handcuffing. They are often CPR and AED certified and they respond to every incident one can imagine. A mall is a huge soft target for terrorists. Mall Security is trained in every type of possible scenario from active shooters to chemical and biological attacks. In some of the malls in more dangerous areas the Mall Public Safety units are armed and trained to use lethal force just like a Cop. In spite of all of this they are disrespected by the Public at large and have even had movies made like Mall Cop with Paul Blart. The Private Security Units often work with and even hire police officers to work with them at certain times and during the holiday season.

In spite of all of the stigmas attached to these real Officers, what is the real advantage with private security from the mall to the campus to the hospital? Unlike the Police these Public Safety Officers know every square inch of every single building on a campus or a mall or a hospital or a stadium and so on. So if a mass casualty incident happens in one of these places the Police will actually rely on these Security Forces. Security will identify the threat, the location of the threat and will even lead them down back corridors or other areas to obtain the best tactical positions to deal with the threat quickly. And this also includes schools. So in effect if the Security force is armed they could end an active shooter incident before the Police ever get to the scene. This equates to potentially, many lives being saved. I personally think that Security Forces are underpaid and that they should all be armed with their total knowledge of the buildings being of such value. In many cases Public Safety Departments have a camera system in use. This is very useful to both Security and Police Officers. Why are they paid so little money when they are placing their lives at risk? It's the same reason I mentioned in the financial system chapter. They are not viewed as valuable assets, they are viewed as a financial drain.

I think it would be useful to discuss how to survive an active shooter scenario that God forbid you find yourself in. These shooters are becoming more and more common. So anyplace that is crowded can be a potential target. So wherever you are you should take notice of every escape route. This gives you the information you need to escape in the direction opposite of the location of the shooter. If here pop pop pop don't hesitate and wonder if you are hearing firecrackers in a mall or a Walmart. Simply assume your hearing gunfire. At this point you start to become frightened. You need to take deep breaths and think clearly to survive.

So in terms of a Walmart where should you go? If the shooter is in the front of the store by the entrance you will want to run to the back of the store. In the back of the store are the employee only areas. Go into this area and continue going towards the back of the building. By law there will be exit signs. Follow these signs as quickly as possible. Once you get outside if there is a tree line of a wooded area go into the woods and continue as far away from the building as possible. If while you are in the store you find yourself being fired upon from behind bend all the way forwards while you run. This will reduce your target profile and any rounds that hit you will be in the legs and buttocks. This prevents bullets from hitting your major organs like the heart and lungs and your head. With your adrenaline you will be able to run with bullets in your legs. If you are bent over running from fire in a parking lot go in between the cars for cover while you run. Once you escape you need to check your bleeding for an arterial hit which could cause you to bleed out. In this case fashion a tourniquet with a belt or whatever is available. Make it tight and get help as soon as possible.

If your in a mall and hear gunfire. Run into the nearest store and go out the back door which will lead to a service corridor with exit signs leading you out to the loading docks. Once outside take a moment and listen for exterior fire as a mall could draw multiple shooters in a soft target terrorist attack. If you hear exterior fire hide anyplace you can and try to find some kind of weapon like a fire extinguisher and attempt to put yourself in an ambush position. This simply consists of any kind of corner a shooter would have to go around. If he comes, then you become the predator and hit him on the head with everything you have (you have about 1 or 2 seconds to do this). Then take his weapon, kill him and remain sheltered in your ambush position. Some or many of you may be asking yourselves, is killing the shooter or terrorist necessary if he's knocked out and I have his rifle? Is this even legal after he's disarmed? The answer is yes for a few reasons. You must assume the shooter is not alone. You must assume the shooter has a second weapon. You must assume that if the shooter is a terrorist that he may strapped with explosives. You must also assume that if he's knocked out he will wake up. What will he do? He will see you not shooting him and probably start approaching you with the intention of getting his rifle back. Once he gets it back he will shoot you dead. This is the harsh reality of surviving against animals.

When the Police ask you later why you shot him, list the things I mentioned above and the Officer will say OK. Basically just explain that it was him or you and that you were fearing for your life. However you must also be aware that you are armed and the Police don't know you. So keep the rifle pointed towards the ground and when you hear the police are coming place the weapon on the ground and lay down with you hands behind your head. It is also a good idea if your in possession of a rifle that you should keep your trigger finger on the trigger guard and not the trigger. You will be full of adrenaline and may accidentally fire the weapon drawing attention to yourself.

If you are an armed person with children do the same thing and shoot any shooter that enters your ambush position, you are obligated to protect your family in my opinion. If you are armed and alone, then you need to find out what you're made of. You can go and kill the shooter or you can try to help get people out as an armed guard. If your hands are shaking that's a good indicator that your not up for the job of going after the shooter or shooters. There is an old saying, never go anywhere without a knife. So if your not armed you should always carry a tactical folder knife of legal length. You may need this if your in the ambush scenario.

If you are forced to shelter in place in some room. Turn your cell phones off and collect weapons that are available. If you are not alone coordinate an ambush by whispering. Also, lock and barricade the door with heavy objects like file cabinets and brace them with objects or even your own weight and turn off the lights. If the door has a window in it, then cover it. A sheet of paper and tape will work fine but find a way. Stay low and silent as bullets go through walls. If the room you are sheltered in has windows with drapes or blinds close them. Wait for the Police and be prepared to go into the prone position when they enter. To them everyone starts off as a suspect and will be cuffed. I hope this information was useful with regards to survival techniques. But the main point is not to be paranoid but to kind of map the places you go and observe the locations of exits as a good habit and know what to do when the shots start ringing out. Perhaps teach this to your teenage kids. On a positive note, it is statistically very unlikely that you will find yourself in a situation like this. The thing to remember is that a survival situation is extreme. You are either the victim or you are a survivor and that may require you to become the predator unfortunately. But on a moral level you have every right to protect yourself and your family from being murdered at the hands of some murderer or terrorist.

Let's take a look at your rights if you are suspected of a crime that you did not commit. Most people feel that they know their rights. You very likely know your miranda rights, the right to remain silent, the right to an attorney and so on (123). But what about your rights if you find yourself in the position of being a suspect of a committed crime that you did not commit. Does this happen? Yes it does. So let's start with with a lower level crime like a fist fight. You get pulled over and you have no idea why. Depending on the severity of the crime the Police will either simply walk up and interview you or they will do a full blown felony stop. A felony stop is when the Police get out of their cars and point their guns at you and start a series of instructions. This may sound familiar to you. "Driver turn off the vehicle". "Driver throw the keys out the window" "Driver exit the vehicle". "Face away from me and slowly walk Backwards". Stop and lay down on the ground". Then they come over and cuff you at gunpoint. This is done when the driver is believed to be armed or some other serious threat.

If you find yourself in a felony stop and you did nothing. You need to do exactly what they say and they will realize your innocence when your identified. Is this possible? Yes it is. Say you drive a red Ford F-150 and just down the road from you a red F-150 was involved in a shooting. The Police are responding and you drive right by them close to the crime scene. They may very well pull you over and do a felony stop, especially if your close to the description of the offender. It's not something that happens constantly but it does happen. Do you have the right to refuse to exit your vehicle. Well, that's your choice but I promise they will remove from your vehicle and your going to be face down on the ground. Your better off complying since you know they are looking for a serious threat. As I mentioned earlier, cops are twitchy and when guns are being pointed at you it's wise to follow instructions.

Let's say it's a far lesser crime like a simple fight/assault or some kind of theft and you did absolutely nothing. Somehow you become a suspect of this crime and they call you up and you to come down to the station for an 'interview'. Do you have to go to them at the Police Department? Not at all. If they had probably cause for an arrest they would simply come and arrest you. They are looking for you to volunteer to come to them on their terms and in their environment. You could do a few things in this case. You could say I haven't done anything but you are more than welcome to come over to my house and we can talk outside or inside depending on your comfort level. If your in an especially bad mood you could just hang up and let them figure out what to do about it. You could tell them that they are being an annoying nuisance and tell them "don't even talk to me without a warrant". If they respond by saying, "this only makes you guilty". You could say "that will change when you locate the real criminal".

Let's say you get pulled over for speeding. The cop writes you a ticket and after he gives it to you he asks you, will you consent to a vehicle search? Translation, will you forfeit your rights voluntarily? If you feel like being cooperative you could allow it since you have nothing to hide. If it were me I would say no. The cop would ask why? I would say "because I don't do volunteer work". But that's just me, I've been told that at times I have a slight attitude. If you are carrying a firearm with a legal carry permit in your State. The cop may ask you at the end after your weapon is returned, "why do you need to carry a gun"? I would say, "because it's my right to do so sir". So my main point here is that you have the right to not consent when asked. Depending on the situation it is up to you if it's worth it or the best move for you to consent. Or if your like me your not consenting to anything for the most part.

Now let's look at the worst type of situation, a member of your own family or a good friend is murdered. This is when things can get very serious for you at an already emotional grief filled time. Your possibly vulnerable and even a little confused. So let's start by assuming you actually did kill a family member. You might as well just turn yourself in. Hardly anyone ever gets away with killing a family member. The people closest to the victim are the first people that murder investigators or detectives look at. Now let's assume you've done nothing wrong. The Police are going to interview you as a potential suspect. They will need an alibi that can be confirmed in order to cross your name off the list of potential suspects. Now if the crime happened 5 days ago you might not even remember where you were and even if you do you may not be able to prove it. If your lucky you were at some appointment during the time that the crime was committed. Or with a friend all day or at work all day and so on.

So let's say you can't provide a provable alibi to satisfy the Police. If they really think your guilty they may try to verbally grill you for hours. This can be attempted when they don't even have the power to detain you yet given their evidence in possession. They would love to get a confession out of you if they think you did it. Police have a legal right to lie to you and present false evidence against you. For example, they might tell you that they have your fingerprints at the crime scene and may say they want a DNA swab because DNA evidence was found at the scene. The very room they bring you in for interrogation is designed to make you uncomfortable. They want your chair to be uncomfortable, they make sure that there are no pictures on the wall. The position you in a corner at times and sit around you so you feel helpless and surrounded. They will begin by establishing a rapport with you. This is just to get you talking and willing to talk.

They will ask irrelevant questions and you will start to feel comfortable being questioned as if this a normal thing or (fundamental assumption). The goal is to manipulate you. So let's say you find yourself in this situation. If it were me, after the first question I would ask "Am I under arrest or being detained against my will?" If the answer is no. Then i would ask, "am I free to go"? The response to this might be a question like, why don't you want to cooperate? This only makes you look guilty if you won't answer a few simple questions. I would then repeat the question "am I free to leave?". At this point there will be a moment of silence more than likely. Then he or she will answer, you are free to go. At that point you simply walk out but don't think for a second that you won't get a parting comment. They might say "don't leave town" or "we will see you soon." Just ignore this irritation they have and walk out the door. They may say that your on the top of the suspect list. I would answer this by saying, "that will change when you do your job and catch the killer of my family member".

So that was a look at voluntary detainment. What happens if your innocent and actually get charged with the crime. This does happen. At this point whatever evidence they have must be weak if they want to interrogate you. This is when things get nasty. They can sit there and lie to you about false evidence that proves your guilty and that you are going away forever. They will say "listen your done, that's a fact, if you confess we might be able to help you". "It's in your best interest to confess if you want a deal". They might ask you to take a polygraph or lie detector test before or after you get charged. I would say no. They would ask why and I would say it's not even admissible in court and I don't do volunteer work. But it's important to understand that homicide detectives are relentless in their quest to bring justice to a murder victim. They will stop at nothing to get a confession and solve a case. So why would you an innocent person want to get grilled and lied to for 20 hours straight when your grieving a family member? Just simply say "I'm not saying a single word to you and I want my lawyer".

As I mentioned earlier a man confessed to killing 150 people in his nursing job using a paralytic drug (24). The District Attorney would not allow him to be held based on only a confession. The reason for this is because it's common knowledge that these interrogations are long and so brutal that innocent people have confessed just to make it stop. The truth is that you don't have to go through this at all. So if you have an alibi that could be verified, great give it to them. If you think you know who did kill your family member then you should tell them everything you know about that. But if your being grilled like a criminal when your innocent. Consent to nothing and don't put yourself through 20 hours of interrogation and lies and manipulation for no reason. If your a cop reading this, you might be saying what a jerk this guy is helping criminals. Actually this is directed at the falsely accused. Besides, we both know that if you as a Cop were arrested, the first thing you would do is lawyer up and maybe call a union representative. You should be telling people this if your honest. These super intense interrogations lasting 20 hours need to end. You either have the evidence to win your case or you don't. Is it really ok to tell people that you have false evidence against them? No it's almost criminal itself.

In defense of the Police and investigative interrogation, it is important to see it's value under the right circumstances. For example, if the Police have an accused murderer in custody, who has given an alibi. Let's assume that the murderer had an accomplice that they have not identified. If the Police want to grill this guy by showing him video and DNA evidence that destroys his alibi and places him at the scene of the murder. They have the murder weapon that has his finger prints on it. It becomes very obvious at this point that they have the right person and this person is not being falsely accused. All of this would be the result of a good and successful investigation. They are not fishing for a confession without direct evidence. It is totally justified to interrogate this person. The guilty party still has a right to an attorney present or to remain silent. Yet it may become necessary to crack this killer and get him to give up his accomplice.

They may even offer a deal of some sort in exchange for the identity of the accomplice. This is all just and fair for the sake of the victim or victims getting justice. The only thing that should be avoided is fishing for a confession with inadequate evidence that could potentially put an innocent person on death row. In all reality, I don't think any homicide detective worth their salt wants this to happen anyway.

CHAPTER 18
'The Directional Paradigm'

At this point you the reader should have an understanding of how our system of government has a major influence on the way people think and the assumptions they operate under. What is a directional paradigm? It is simply the direction that humanity has gone over the centuries. Much of this paradigm revolves around the priorities that we as a human race have established. This does vary from culture to culture. However, in spite of your culture or race, there is still a paradigm that is under the surface of all races and cultures. To see this paradigm and its current state we must travel back to the beginning in the formation of the so called 'industrial revolution'.

The industrial revolution (124) began in England sometime around 1850. The actual precursors to this so called revolution go as far back to the 1700's. What basically happened in my opinion was the invention of the steam engine. These steam engines produced the first trains. That train was important for transporting products and people. Yet the highly important thing that happened was the use of these steam engines to be used in what became factories. The first major advancement in factories was the ability to produce textiles on a grand scale. Before this, clothing or (textiles) were made by hand. Once the steam engine was introduced to human paradigms, it produced an opportunity for others. That opportunity was to invent machines that mimicked the old fashioned hand looms for creating cloth. So what was the motivation of these inventors? The motivation was money. Now we had both rich factory owners and jobs for the common person. This paradigm did not exist in the previous history of the world.

This industrial revolution quickly spread to the United States. As time passed this new factory and mass production paradigm evolved to produce more and more products. Factories made shoes and socks along with the creation of mass produced lumber. Mass produced lumber allowed us to build new types of homes and factories. The mass production of steel was also a massive advancement born of this revolution. Now guns and every other thing made of metal could be mass produced. In time other metals would be created ranging from aluminium to higher alloys. Eventually the non steam fuel powered combustion engine was invented. The invention of the gasoline fueled combustion engine gave birth to the oil industry. At this point, inventors were highly motivated to take advantage of this brave new world changing at the speed of light. This can only be compared to what is called a geometric progression (125).

In a nuclear bomb two round pieces of uranium or plutonium are smashed together with explosives and one atom splits another releasing a great deal of energy. This starts a chain reaction, one atom splits another leading to 2 and then 4 and then 8, 16, 32, 64, 128, 236 and on it goes very quickly into the billions or trillions. This happens so fast in a nuclear bomb that it creates an explosion that mimics the sun and as we all know it's powerful enough to level a city. I'm sure a nuclear bomb is more complicated than this but you get the point. Henry Ford questioned the age old paradigm of people using horses to travel and transport goods. He used the combustion engine to create an automobile. It had great advantages, the operator was sheltered from the environment like the horse drawn buggy and as a consequence we needed gas stations. The military invented tanks and better rifles and handguns along with artillery pieces. Eventually the airplane was invented and another industry followed which eventually led to fighter planes and commercial air travel. All of these advancements led to other advancements and more products invented by the ambitious who wanted to make a fortune.

Eventually scientists and engineers were crucial in the development of advancements. And two world wars created a necessity for new advancements. Things like canned food and the microwave oven are a direct result of war. In time scientist in the military and NASA saw a need for computing devices. In the beginning of this quest a computer used spinning reels of tape for computation. A computer in the beginning took an entire floor of a building to house all of the equipment needed to do simple computations. In time the microprocessor was invented and this was a massive advancement. With the microprocessor, computers became much smaller and created another market with computers being sold to businesses and the public at large. These computers needed what is called an operating system. This created a need filled by Bill Gates with the Windows Operating System. Apple was also a computer operating system inventor and also sold computers. In the beginning Windows won this competition between operating systems being sold on the open market. Once computers were made with an effective operating system, we needed an internet for computers to communicate in. In time we saw the development of the cell phone which evolved to the smartphone. Your smartphone is probably several thousand times more powerful a computer then the computer used in the first lunar lander. The internet initially relied on slow broadband over the telephone lines. We all had phone modems back when Windows 95 came to the market. Now we have high speed internet and are on the verge of 5G which is supposed to take us to the next level.

We have also seen a massive market in the advancement of medicine. In the past if you suffered a wound and it got infected, that might have been it for you. Now we have antibiotics for that problem. We have huge advancements in cancer treatments and anesthesia for surgeries. If you cut yourself you can go to the pharmacy (another resulting market), and buy antibiotic ointment with some bandaids. You are in fact doing what was only dreamed of 200 years ago. We can have a pandemic however with things like the H1N5 bird flu potentially going airborne at some point. We have cured Hepatitis C and things like CAT Scans are all high tech advancements in the world of medicine. Our current life expectancy is around 79-80 years as a result of medical advancement. The list goes on and on. This is just my take on how things developed in our directional paradigm.

When conspiracy theorists view this sudden geometric progression I just described, they say it's just not possible. They believe that the only way this could have happened so quickly is that we obtained this technology from crashed alien spaceships (126). Do I believe in aliens? Anything is possible, but in all truth I just don't know. If they are here and visiting, they are not making contact with us, so I really couldn't care less. If they land in my backyard and hand me a pill that makes my body 20 years old again and I will live for millions of years then I will care very much. But in examining the evidence I believe that we have undergone a technological geometric progression that was all started by an English man named Thomas Savery who invented the steam engine and was born in 1650 (127). If you watch a TV show about UFO's the main issue of amazement with this possibility of aliens is of course the technology they must possess. This a little piece of evidence that technology permeates the minds of the people. This of course does not list every single advancement in technology since the beginning of the Industrial Revolution. These are just my own observations.

Is this technology paradigm a bad thing? No not at all. We have come a very long way in a very short period of time. Quality of life for many people in the world is much better than our ancestors. So what is the directional paradigm that we live in? The directional paradigm is the ever expanding development of technology. As we all know, people care about things like social media websites. We love our smartphones and online shopping. We want that high definition television and those first person shooter video games. We now have ambulances that will come and rescue us if we have a medical emergency and the Police if we are in danger. But in essence for this technological expansion to continue it requires order in our society. The job of law and order falls on the government and the Police. Countries like China do not seek so much to invade us in this time. They want to be the premier financial and military superpower in the world. If you look to our South you see Mexico, which in all reality is a third world country.

The technology paradigm creates plenty of Billionaires like Bill Gates who is worth over 100 billion dollars (74). Does that make him a bad person? Not at all, as we discussed earlier, we need Capitalism and must reject the failure known as Socialism. The directional paradigm of technology has advanced technology, but have human beings and human thinking advanced on an equal level to technology? The answer is no, not even close in my opinion. Let's examine how much less we the people have advanced in comparison to technology.

We live in a time of polarized division as we discussed earlier. The people are divided on the political level and the current adversarial paradigm can be blamed for the system we are influenced by. We almost seem to love confrontation and division. This drama of division is so accepted that it's just the normal course of business as we also discussed earlier. A new system that is non adversarial and a fair compensation act would preserve capitalism and decrease poverty while we improve the quality of life. Political division and the system does have a massive influence on us. However, the division goes much deeper as a result.

When I was young, if you would have told me that in 2019 or 2020 and going forward, that we would still have homeless people. I would have said no way that will never happen. We will have by then, eliminated homelessness completely. Yet as seen in the media major cities like Los Angeles and San Francisco we see tent cities of the homeless stretching down the sidewalk. People are living under bridges and this is happening all over the country. The news media reports that people are defecating in the street and regular people are trying not to step on the massive numbers of syringes on the sidewalk. Is this the best we can do? Of course not, however, in the current paradigm, taking care of the poor is just another drain on the system. Many of these people are mentally ill or even mentally ill veterans (128).

We have the so called 'Opioid Crisis', (129) we hear reports of drug dealers cutting Heroin with Fentanyl causing huge numbers of overdoses. Many Police Officers carry Narcan with them on duty to treat overdose victims. Some of these cases require multiple doses of Narcan to reverse the effects of Opioid overdoses (130). New designer drugs come out on a regular basis. The estimated amount of money spent on illegal drugs in the United States every year is nearly 150 billion dollars (131). What can we attribute all of this drug addiction to? Most people simply blame the drugs, especially prescription painkillers which are prescribed by doctors. Some States have even made money with lawsuits against large pharmaceutical companies. In terms of human thinking and the examination of it I see a different problem. People are miserable in many cases. If you are the poor and depressed and mentally ill in many cases you may just simply need to escape reality with Heroin. The problem with Opioids is that they work in treating general misery. For the so called 'junky' as we like to label them, being a drug addict is the only way to tolerate life's misery.

Once people are addicted to Heroin it is almost impossible to get off of it. I was watching the TV show Drugs Inc, they had this drug dealer wearing a mask talking about Heroin (132). This dealer said, "Heroin is the most addictive drug in the world, I don't care what anyone tells you, once your on this, it's for life". Like every drug dealer he says the same old justifying thing. If I'm not selling this someone else will. This is true, yet a drug dealer is a killer who sells poison to people suffering from some form of human misery. The blaming of pharmaceutical pain killers is resulting in a sort of barbarism that is endorsed by our government health care system. Depending on what State you live in, you might break your leg and only be given pain meds for three or four days. Is that reasonable? Not at all, it is a sort of hysterical reaction to a supposed crisis that can only be solved by taking legitimate pain management and villainizing it. This is the fear of the great opioid epidemic. Pain management is one of the most merciful and civilized things of the modern age. So if you break your leg I guess you need to go out and buy a bottle of bourbon like the year 1880. Then again in 1880 opium could be bought at the pharmacy. Laudanum was a mixture of opium and alcohol and resulted in many overdoses back then (133).

So this is nothing new, opium dens existed a thousand years ago or more. In essence the real crisis is both mental illness and simple human misery. Even people who are worth millions of dollars experience misery leading to drug addiction. I've seen many celebrities on TV talking about how they had to go to rehab and then relapsed or even got arrested as their life fell apart. So why in this directional paradigm of technological advancement are people leaning on alcohol and drugs to cope with life's misery and problems of the mind? It is because the direction of our thinking in this directional paradigm of technology has no effect on how we 'choose to think'. The paradigm shift of giving the power to the people would give people a sense of purpose and involvement and would provide some help with this problem of human misery and mental illness. If we create a non adversarial society that also gives people the opportunity to make a decent living it would help but it would not completely fix the addiction problem in my opinion.

There is talk recently in the media of declaring Mexican drug cartels terrorist organizations (134). Is this a reasonable comparison to traditional forms of terrorism from Islamic terrorist to domestic terrorist? There are two perfect similarities in my view. For example we have the Mexican cartels in places like Juarez Mexico who kill people in the most brutal ways one can imagine just like Isis. Yet that may not be enough to justify taking out these cartels on a military level. The biggest reason to compare them to terrorist is the simple fact that they are killing more American citizens than other terrorists organizations bar far. Many thousands of Americans have died as a direct result of these drug cartels in both Mexico and other countries. We have heard the term 'the war on drugs' for many years. Yet if we want to end all of this poisoning death going on in our country we need a literal military war on drugs. Our military special forces and the intelligence community are more than capable of doing this. Part of the problem in my opinion is that half of the Police and politicians in Mexico are corrupt and on the payroll of these cartels. To put it simply to them, we should advise these corrupt police and politicians on one thing. They are either going to be designated as a terrorist or paid informant, their choice.

So let's say we do this and we wipe out every drug cartel and their perspective crops off the face of the Earth. Will it fully solve the problem? No it won't, this is because people will try to fill this drug vacuum with domestic drugs like methamphetamines. We could call them domestic terrorists but in the end none of this will cure human misery and human thinking. One thing that creates human misery is poverty. We would eliminate some or even most of this poverty with a Fair Compensation Act. Yet we have other cultural paradigms in place that increase human misery and criminal activity for that matter. I have interviewed people who have told me that they were born into a gang and they were proud of it. What is a gang? In my opinion there are a variety of types. We have small inner city gangs that occupy a single block or several blocks. We national level gangs like the Crips and Bloods. These gangs are big and exist both in and out of prisons. We have some white supremacist gangs like Naziz and KKK members. We have Biker Gangs (oh excuse me, MC's or motorcycle clubs). Translation criminal gangs that like motorcycles. All of these gangs make money on drugs and in the case of Biker Gangs they run a lot of illegal guns and drugs. We have multiple bikers gangs that fight with each other like the Hells Angels versus the Mongols and the Outlaws.

So the problem is not just the cartels it is the criminal distribution systems already in place. If you are born in a state of poverty and you are raised in an environment of violence and gang activity, your at a disadvantage. People in this position can escape this paradigm but most will not. Some go into the military and create a life for themselves. For the most part people born into this world will integrate right into it in my opinion. In this paradigm you are judged by how 'hard' you are. If you want to be a member of the gang as a teenager you will get beat in. This is simply being punched and stomped for specific period of time as a right of passage to toughen you up and embrace violence in life. In biker gangs you become a probationary member or 'probi'. During this period you are the handmaiden of the gang. You guard the bikes while everyone is in the bar and do whatever they want at all times. Eventually you get your 'patch' and are a full fledged member of the gang.

What is the appeal in this life, and why would anyone want to go through this? When you grow up in a paradigm you become part of the system as we have discussed. Why would an eighteen year old gang members want to work at Walmart? These gang members can earn several thousand dollars per week selling drugs. They would rather risk being shot by a rival gang member or going to prison for most of their life because that is what it means to be 'hard'. Beneath all of this paradigm is the simple human need for a person to feel like they are a part of something. This gang culture paradigm is also an example of tribal behavior. What can be done to stop all of this? It seems almost impossible to stop. Why is it legal to be a gang member? I suppose it could fall under the right to assembly. I believe we need two things to fix this paradigm of criminal violence, drug sales and murder. The first thing we need is the simple creation of a law which outlaws the both the existence and membership of a known criminal organisation. So if your a gang member at all you go to jail. Is this too harsh? When you consider the fact that 40-60 people are shot every weekend just in Chicago in gang drug related activity it's not. This happens all over the country all of the time. This also would apply to prison gangs. You can be convicted of this as an inmate who is part of the Arien Brotherhood or any other gang.

The other thing we need to eliminate this problem is opportunities for gang members to make an actual living wage. People need to survive, it's the most basic instinct. The paradigm of a Fair Compensation Act would provide many opportunities for poor. The destroying of drug cartels removes the product that gangs and drug dealers sell. The Anti Criminal Organization Act would reduce gangs on the streets and the prisons. The fair compensation act would provide the ability to survive and have food and shelter. We will always have crime but the culture of crime can be gradually eliminated if we take all of the needed steps in combination to replace the drug and crime culture paradigm. With a Non Adversarial System of Government the poor would be participating in the process on an equal level with every other free members of our society. In other words, we would all have an equal voice.

This brings me to the paradigm of racism. For thousands of years people have discriminated against other people for a variety of reasons. During the Crusades (134) Islam was attempting to subjugate the world under the banner of Islam and Sharia law. The recent ISIS (5) caliphate was an attempt to form another empire in the name of Islamic subjugation to the law of the Prophet. This is a religious discrimination with the goal to force all of us to converte or die. We of course crushed this so call caliphate out of necessity. Hitler felt that exterminating the Jews would aid him in the creation of the so called aryan race (135). Today's neo nazi groups still want this nonesense. The Soviet Union wanted to take over the world and force us all to become communist and the government would provide you with everything and control everything. This is a discrimination against anyone who is not a communist on a systemic level. This communist paradigm seems to have imploded in on itself. Yet China is a communist country. The difference with China is that they have communist rule over the people, yet they participate in global capitalism by making and selling everything in the world.

The main issue of racism today is based on skin color. It seems that skin color is relevant and we are supposed to be divided into skin color (races) that are separated one from another. Each skin color group discriminates against the other. They have racial slurs within each skin color group to both separate and discriminate against each other. Black people originate from Africa for the most part. Hispanic People originate from South America and perhaps Spain. Asian People originate from China, Japan, and the arctic circle with the Eskimos. Middle Eastern People come from the middle east. Indian People come from India. Native Americans come from right here. White people come from Europe and Russia. They all have various complexions and they look different from the other groups in spite of the fact that they are all human beings.

So what do we call this? For one thing it is a great example of tribal behavior. Tribal behavior is contrary to the human thinking that is required for an advanced human civilization. One thing that has always puzzled me was the choice of skin color as the thing chosen by everyone to discriminate against. Why not discriminate against eye color? Why not discriminate against the size of ones ears or nose? For that matter, why don't we just discriminate against the color of people's shoes. On a scientific level I can say with a fair amount of certainty that human skin is human skin regardless of the color. Some of this racial paradigm is based on the enslavement of black people by white people in the fairly distant past and the mistreatment of black people during the days of segregation. Today we still have black people being profiled by some people. Yet if black people want to hate white people it is perfectly fine in the current paradigm. Some have called this reverse discrimination. Discrimination is discrimination if we are honest. And discrimination is something that comes from any skin color against any other skin color.

Do we really even want this to end? Do some skin color groups want it to end more than others? Well if your some kind of Nazi Muffin covered with tatoos from the third reich you want discrimination to increase and start some sort of race war. But when we step back from our complexions, we can all see that we share the race of humans. Who else wants us to be divided into these races of skin color and national origin? That would be our political leaders who run for office. They don't simply want the votes of the American People. They want the black vote, the Hispanic vote, the highly educated white female vote, the christian vote the Jewish vote the asian vote and so forth. So how on Earth do we fix this problem of racism and the division it causes between us? We already have laws for hate crimes. Yet we are still divided as though it's just in our genes to discriminate.

This problem is not in our genes. Once again let's take a look at the contradictions in racism. We all work together and seem to get along just fine in most workplaces. Why do we get along at work and then go home and speak racist talk in private? It's against the rules to discriminate in the workplace. So if we wish to stay gainfully employed we must be what I will call race neutral. Race Neutral sounds pretty good to me as a position to take in life on a philosophical level. Another contradiction is the NFL. How many millions of white people spend most of their Sundays watching football? Do they sling racial slurs the whole time at the black football players? No they don't. In fact they view black and white players as amazing athletes. Take a player from the past, Laurence Taylor (136). This guy was black, but he was one of the greatest defensive players to ever play the game. He was just vicious and actually became a legend as the guy who ended Joe Thiesman's career as a quarterback after he broke his leg. His leg broke so badly that his career as quarterback ended right there in that one infamous Lawrence Taylor tackle. Did anyone care that he was black? No not all, he was simply Laurence Taylor. So why was this the case? Why did racism not affect Laurence Taylor as a black man? The reason was because he was great as a football legend. So in essence his skin became a non issue and one hundred percent irrelevant.

Race neutral is more than just a phrase that sounds nice. It is a realization that the color of other people's skin needs to and must, simply become a non issue. Many people already embrace this whether they realize it or not. So how can this be accomplished? The biggest factor in this Race Neutral paradigm being born is that each race or culture must teach this to one another and their children. Our leaders and members of the so called media could embrace race neutrality and still be politically correct. If we are going to be educated by our so called leaders (which will never be their job) they should embrace race neutrality as a philosophy that treats all people with equal respect and dignity. If this is taught and embraced it will become a paradigm all its own. Can we do this? Is the world ready for this and all of the other paradigms we have discussed? I'm sure someone back in the days of our founding fathers asked a similar question. They may have asked, is the world ready for a country without a King? Is the world ready for a government of the people. I would imagine that the answer from the founding fathers was simply. "If not now, then when"?

Chapter 19

'Education'

Education is both a simple and complicated subject. As children we go to kindergarten and as we progress through elementary school we learn the ever so important basics. We learn to read and write, we learn basic math. Then we go through middle school and high school learning a lot of things from algebra to history and all of the rest. Is a basic education important? Of course it is, we need to be able to read and write and do basic math. Although a younger family member of mine was doing math in a new way. It seemed like an alien code to me as I watched in a state of sheer surprise. It was as if 10 steps were added to each math problem that was solved. I asked my young relative about it and he said, "I don't know, that's just the way we do it". I have no idea what the benefit is in doing math in a new way. I will just have to trust that there is some good reason for it. Perhaps it helps students in progressing to higher levels of math up to advanced calculus. Or perhaps it is just some stupid new way to do math that over complicates things.

Once we graduate from highschool, the entire world of education changes dramatically. If you go to an Ivy League college it will cost you a fortune in student loans. That is unless you have wealthy parents who simply pay for it all. College professors are not just in the business of teaching you your major or the subject of the class of your in. Professors commonly use their position of teacher to further their own beliefs and their political theology. They add their own views to the course in order to truly enlighten the student. The wish to bring them into the world of enlightenment and advanced thinking. What you learn with regards to political theology (as I call it), is probably different from State to State. I'm sure that we have both liberal and conservative professors.

Progressive education as we discussed earlier is the education of moral relativism (14) which again is the notion that morality is not a black and white issue. Morality in this system is decided by the individual and it can range from a Priest in the seminary to a new age kid in a liberal college practicing Satanism. It's all the same thing depending on your personal opinion. Yet we see these students in our current paradigm as the people who will be our future leaders. I noticed over the years that a great many of Congress People are lawyers or former prosecutors. One would think this makes perfect sense. After all they are law makers, lawyers know about the law so they are the logical choice.

Yet as we discussed the Adversarial System of Government is based on rhetoric and deception of the masses. Lawyers are professionals at spinning the truth and manipulating people and groups of people. So from the standpoint of an adversarial system of government, these lawyers are the people who naturally evolve into office. They have no problem producing charismatic campaign speeches and as a result of this they get elected based on who is the best manipulator with the best rhetorical deception. This millennial generation is a new and totally different generation than anything we have seen in the past generations.

Millennials (118) are truly trying attempting to change the existing paradigms in what I must assume is a result of the teachings of their professors. In this new way of thinking we learn all about gender identity and so many new priorities like misogynism and xenophobia are not just ideals to millenials. They are the evil works of the prior generations which need to be simply rolled over and forced into green new deals. Then we have the life threatening climate crisis that will cause the end of the world in as little as nine years. I saw a football game protest between Yale and Harvard last week. Before the game could begin hundreds of young protesters stormed the football field to force climate change awareness (137). Well I guess if you believe the world is going to end and nobody cares. Your going to do whatever you have to in order to survive the coming apocalypse. Pretty soon all of our coastal cities will be underwater and Florida I'm assuming will simply disappear into the ever rising ocean.

On the surface these revolutionary millennials sound like the sort of people who are gearing up for a war and they will be heard. They sound like green warriors mustering their forces in preparation for the next level of the movement. These brave souls are going to save us all from ourselves. Yet if some of them get questioned by the Police or Campus Security they become so frightened that they become literally traumatized. Even in the most professional and respectful of conversations with an authority figure they may need to go to an assigned safe place to decompress. They want to feel safe at all times and anything that feels unsafe will scar them for life and they may need therapy. So these students are paying hundreds of thousands of dollars to be influenced into a state of mind that lives in fear. The fear of a mass shooting brings them all together to demand that the evil .223 black rifle (28) that is the most powerful weapon of war in the history of humanity.

Truth be told a .223 is a glorified .22 caliber round. The paradigm of the .223 semi automatic rifle being the lunatic mass shooters weapon of choice is actually not such a bad thing. Have you ever noticed that most of the .223 shootings produce as many wounded as they do fatalities? We are lucky that they don't choose the AR-10 which has a 20 round magazine of .308 high power rifle rounds. The gun has very little recoil and will likely result in death for anyone hit from the waist up. So let's keep that .223 AR-15 on the top evil list of guns that kill people the best.

In spite of this new generation of millenials we shouldn't be too hard on them and calling them snowflakes. Let us take another look at them as victims. They are victims of the ultra liberal extremism that is engulfing the Democratic Party. This is not about bashing the left it is simply an observation of the new direction that the Democrats are going in. These millennials are eating this sort of college rhetorical brainwashing like candy. They are just victims of this emerging paradigm that we are all witnessing as they try to recreate the country into a socialist republic (32).

Colleges are not free, therefore they are businesses. They charge vast amounts of money to provide students with an education. In spite of this we see a little under fifty percent of students dropping out of college (138). They flunk out and as a result the college makes far less money then they would if the number was 90 percent success for instance. So what on Earth are they thinking with regards to the business model when they are losing that much money? Are they taking into account that people learn in different ways? Not at all, the curriculum is set in stone. As a consequence, what you see is the ascension of a certain group of people who I can only describe as book smart. These people are not bad people, they are just people who have brains that are wired to read material and possess good memorization skills. In other words they remember what they read more than others, therefore they tend to pass tests and then succeed in graduating if they apply themselves. This seemingly insane business model of fifty percent success is considered a good thing by the colleges.

This separates the smartest people from the stupid people and allows the graduate to ascend to the coveted level of elitism (139). This elitism is so important to colleges that it is worth losing fifty percent of prospective profits. After these so called elite people among the idiots graduate from college they go on to their perspective fields and obtain jobs in high ranking positions. These positions include leadership positions in companies regardless of the fact that they may have no leadership qualities whatsoever. These elite people go into journalism with these elite progressive ideas and they control the narrative that you mentally ingest. Of course these elite people also end up leading us in Congress and other political positions on the State and local levels. And of course they also become college professors thus perpetuating this cycle of elitism for generations to come. Is leadership something that is taught in schools? They do teach business management, but does this actually teach a person effective leadership skills? No it does not, in fact if you look at our millennial generation they seem to be encouraged to not even face their own fears. They are basically told to hide from fear in a safe place.

When a person is developing into an adult or an adult leader they must have some level of basic human character. One quality of a leader with character is the ability to overcome one's own fears. A leader must also be able to view the world and their job as a leader from a global perspective. Leaders need to view things from fifty thousand feet and make management decision. These management decisions of a leader should be evident by the respect level of their subordinates. A great leader will learn that empowering their subordinates will be far more effective than demeaning them and being on a power trip. When you empower your people they will enjoy what they are doing and they will respect you a great deal for being that rare leader amongst leaders. These are qualities that are prioritised in the military, or in fortunate cases a person is raised by their parents to become a leader.

Is our current system teaching and encouraging leadership in our people? Not at all, yet this current millennial generation will, in time, become our leaders and run this country. This notion of a Non Adversarial System of Government will both produce leadership qualities and global thinking. If the people are making the choices via participation in every issue they will think globally and they will think as leaders. This paradigm of empowering the people will change people's thinking. The difference is that we will be teaching people by setting them free from manipulation and lies. Currently the people are educated via manipulation and deception and rhetoric. When the people become free from influence and manipulation they themselves by default will become the thinkers. The paradigm we have right now is quite close to being literal brainwashing of the masses on a grand scale. This brainwashing may not be the intention within the paradigm but merely a symptom of it.

The question becomes what is education, teaching and learning? Once again to figure this out we must examine all of the information in the existing paradigm. Education in my opinion is the simple act of learning something new that you didn't know before. This is currently done by lecturing of the information by the teacher and reading the books provided to the student. This includes homework and ultimately a test which the student either passes or fails. Teaching is the act of (successfully) providing students with the information they need to learn. Teachers operate under a curriculum that applies to all of the students in the same way. So given the fact that we have one style of curriculum we should examine the different ways that people learn. Is it just one way that people learn? In my research I have found seven different ways that people learn. Here is a list, ,Visual (Spatial), Aural (Auditory), Verbal (linguistic), Physical (Kinesthetic), Logical (Mathematical), Social (Interpersonal), Solitary (Intrapersonal) (140). I would personally add to this list the way I seem to learn which seems to be **conceptual**. I see the world through concepts and must understand the entire concept of something before I can fully learn it. What we see here is the simple fact that people are wired in many different ways when they learn. Does the current educational paradigm take this fact that we all learn in different ways and apply it to teaching? No they do not. I can understand that you can't make a curriculum in a single form that applies to every style of learning.

However, we must also examine this notion of testing and teaching. As it stands we have a teacher or professor who is in charge of educating you. You must pass the test or final in order to succeed and graduate. The concept of testing on a pass fail basis is worth questioning. When I trained people in certain tactical courses I was required to pass an instructors course. Some of this course was book work and written tests,. The majority of the course was simple physical one on one training to learn how to teach people to use various tools like pepper spray or handcuffing for example. These instructors over the years varied in teaching styles but in the end they were less worried about written tests and more worried about your skill sets. This was due to the simple fact that I would be training people to use these tools in dangerous situations. The instructors for the most part wanted you to demonstrate to them that you both understand it and that you could do it. Once you proved to them physically that you could do it they were satisfied that you have been educated.

Over the course of time I taught many people many different things ranging from Spray and Cuffs to self defense, tasers and effective leadership skills to supervisors who were my subordinates. Report writing and photography of incident scenes and the list goes on and on. The more I educated people the more I realized that people will learn things much more easily when you remove pressure from the education experience. Once the pass fail pressure is removed from the equation people just become sponges soaking up the relevant information. I learned that some people learn differently from others and I figured out how to teach them because that was my job as the teacher. Teachers in Public Schools and institutions of higher education do not view the pressure placed on students a factor at all. If you pass you pass and if you fail you fail. They get paid either way and that is part of education paradigm.

Is it possible to change how children and adults are educated?

Of course it is, we must remember that we can do anything we want. One good place to start is this notion of elitism (139). Within the elite we have people who are at the top of their class. These people I suppose can be called the super elite. Elitism is simple arrogance and a basis of the ancient class system that still exist. Some people are just better than others, they are more important than others. If you are a rich person you are far superior to others. Yet when some form of chaos comes into a crowded place like an active shooter scenario, everybody becomes equal immediately. I refer to this affect as things getting real. When things get real we find out if the elite billionaire has more character than the Marine who did three combat tours. We find out what we are really made of when things get real. When things are not real people tend to simply assume they are elite if they fall into that so called category. How can we remove elitism from the paradigm in education and society at large? We already know that a Non Adversarial System would put people on an equal level in the system. This is important but it does not remove elitism from education.

Removing elitism requires eliminating the things that qualify a person for this so called elite status. As it stands now we grade students from A to F or a number score from 0 to 100. Why not just use a system of pass fail? That would reduce elitism partially but it would not eliminate it outright. Perhaps we need to change the curriculum and the grading system simultaneously. The classroom could become a place that never gives up on the student. No more pass or fail system at all. The purpose of this is too simply ascertain that the student has learned the material to an adequate level. If the student has not learned the information to an adequate level the teachers or professors aid would be responsible for fixing that. They would ask a series of questions and each one that is answered incorrectly would be addressed by teaching the right answer to the student. The best way to do this in a large classroom is not something I have invented. Perhaps small groups of students working together in study groups is a helpful suggestion. But with this I will happily admit my limitations and simply leave the creation of a better class format to education experts and professors. You're the smartest people in the room, I'm sure you can come up with something.

Once the appropriate level of information is learned either on a students own merits or with the help of the teachers aid you don't get a so called grade. You simply have a box checked next to your name on a list that says information learned. You simply are marked and graded as learned or not learned. If not learned then you get help to score the learned status which is not considered elite. After all the point of education is for people to learn. And once you have learned your grade will be learned and only learned by all equally. If a person in college is simply not able to obtain the learned check box in spite of endless efforts that's when the student is done. But that does not mean that they are some sort of looser. It simply means that the student is in the wrong field. So in order to become a Lawyer you must learn much different information than a person in technical school learning to be a diesel mechanic. Some diesel mechanics can not be lawyers and some lawyers could never repair a diesel engine. With the fair compensation act one job would be no more important than the other.

So in effect we remove all of the pressure of the pass fail system and we replace it with the simple idea that the person has learned the information. Students could even be tested to establish how they learn and what areas they would be likely to excel in. A college degree comes without any grade point average. You simply get a degree that says that in the area of History for example you have been educated. So what is the motivation to excel as a student under this system? People will be motivated by the fact that the better they are at whatever they learn the better chance they will get the best job. Employers who hire people will need to be shown by the applicant that they have the skills they are advertising with the degree. So if the diesel mechanic goes for a job interview, he or she will not just need to talk a good game in an interview. The applicant will need to take apart and reassemble some part of a diesel engine chosen by the employer. This will apply to everything from the Lawyers to Doctors to Teachers and Professors and Brain Surgeons. Everyone will have their skills evaluated in the job interview by the employer. Nobody will be elite yet competition will exist based solely on your level of skill.

Will some people be considered more skilled than others? Yes, we will always have competition on some level. Yet we can remove the the so called elite paradigm from the system. Leadership can be taught to our leaders and we the people may choose people who are not lawyers to go into Congress. We may prefer people with life experience and leadership experience to be in positions of leadership. We may prefer teachers and professors who are experts at teaching people in many ways depending on how they learn. This will produce an un-elite system of education that will produce a number far better than fifty percent failure. Perhaps we can strive for eight percent failure. And the students who don't make it in a specific field will be reimbursed for the remaining time in the semester they have not used if they decide to drop out. With the birth of online colleges we will likely see this expand substantially. In time I believe that online education will cost 90 percent less than regular colleges. We may even see online education infused into Public Education in some way. Perhaps if a student is having trouble in a certain course they can go online in school and get help from an online tutor ten States away. This system of education I'm writing here may not be the best with regard to structure. The main idea is the elimination of elitism and the recognition of the fact that people learn in different ways. In an age when 'everyone gets a trophy', we have only taken legitimate competition out of the picture in sports. The real trophy we need to eliminate is the trophy of elitism and all its tentacles reaching through our modern society.

Now that we have covered the education system we must ask another question. Is education the only way to learn? Education in schools is only the beginning of how people learn. In my opinion we need to explore what we learn in terms of life experience and how we become wise people. Wisdom is not something you can learn in a college course. It comes from life experiences and the will a person has to improve themselves. Self improvement is a choice that can only be made by the individual person. You have to seek out wisdom and you have to have a foundation upon which you build yourself into a better and wiser person. I have spoken to people making minimum wage who are wiser than people I have spoken to with masters degrees. Who would you rather spend three hours talking about life with?. An older, say, seventy year old guy who is very wise. He works in a convenience store, or a corrupt US Senator who speaks like a commercial and smiles like a toothpaste commercial? I will take the guy in the convenience store every time.

In my journey through life, I have learned that nothing can transcend experience when it comes to education. That's not to say that every older person is wise and that wisdom can not be obtained by the young. Some people, in fact many people reach a certain point in personal development and just stop for some reason. They seem to be content in settling for the idea of saying "that's just the way I am". If a person does this they simply just stay at whatever level of wisdom they have if any at all. But I believe that any person who is not mentally disabled can become more than they are if they choose to do so. Should the quest for personal growth span our entire lives? I think it should. I've personally noticed that older people tend to become 'set in their ways'. Not all do this but many do. I for one have decided to never be that man who just stops learning and advancing mentally to the next level. As a basic philosophy this can be taught in schools and by parents. Many people use religion to advance as a human being. They desire to become the person that God wants them to be in their spiritual development.

These wise people are the best hope for humanity. Yet wisdom can be lost in the fog of things like materialism or elitism or general wealth. Once we realize that we are not better than anybody else we can learn a multitude of other things. The rich cling to their possessions in some cases when materialism takes root their minds. Yet a wise person understands the simple wise concept that in the end you can't take anything with you. Rich people can realize this as well. Some of the mega rich billionaires become philanthropist as they get older and retire with this massive sum of money. It is almost as if they realize their own mortality and may even feel guilty about having so much money when others are suffering in poverty in my view. Did these rich people always feel this way? It's possible for a younger billionaire to be a philanthropist but it is far less likely. The young and wealthy seem more consumed by the idea of acquiring wealth and that ever important elitism status placing themselves above the rest of the population. People want to achieve so called greatness and they often hunger for power.

We see this hunger for Power in the tyrants of the world and the tyrants of History like Adolf Hitler. Hitler was so power hungry that he wanted to establish an entire global Arien Empire based on ideals that can only be described as insane. He believed that the master race was a real thing and he formed an extremely powerful military. Many people see the technology of the Nazi's armies as superior to ours. In many cases it was. Our standard Sherman Tanks were a joke compared the Panzer Tiger tank. When D day was approaching Hitler's best General Erwin Rommel advised Hitler that we would likely invade in exact places that we did. Rommel wanted to move all of his heavy armoured divisions to places like Omaha Beach and the other invasion points of the D Day invasion of Europe. Hitler in his arrogance thought he knew better than Rommel and ordered him to maintain his positions. Hitler assumed that we would invade in Caleta France. So the simple ego problem that Hitler had forced him to micro manage his own military and make foolish choices. If Rommel had in fact moved his armies to the shore lines of our actual invasion points, we would have likely been repelled in the invasion of Europe. We would all be speaking German right now. Hitler also decided to invade Russia when he should have invaded England. England was our staging point before invading Europe. We all amassed in England then crossed the English channel to invade Europe. If Hitler had ignored Russia he could have taken England and leapfrogged right over to Canada or South America and gradually worked his way into the United States. That's not to say that Hitler would have won in the end, but then again he might have done it. This is all my own personal opinion.

So Hitler was a powerful and Charismatic politician in my opinion who wanted to be Alexander the Great. In the process he used racist philosophy with his so called master race to kill six million Jews in his twisted quest. Hitler can only be described as a truly evil visionary. But was he a wise man in his decision making? Fortunately for us the answer is no. Hitler made multiple errors that allowed us decimate his vast armies. Since Hitler decided to invade Russia and take on the likes of an evil dictator like Joseph Stalin he was decimated by both the United States and Russia. Not very wise of him at all. In our military we had some very brilliant Generals like George Patton. He was a fast moving army that successfully rolled right over the Nazi armies with inferior tanks and the advantage of sheer numbers of troops and tanks.

The world took very close notice of what this country of ours is capable of when we fully commit to a war. In my opinion we learned lessons from Hitler having superior technology. We decided that we must always be at the top of the food chain with regards to military technology. This was and is a wise decision. Russia tries to keep up in the so called arms race but they will continue to fail. The United States military has the smartest people in the room developing weapons that boggle the mind in their ability to destroy the enemy. If we are honest as a government we would admit that the best and greatest technology is reserved for the military. Much of this technology may be top secret. On one hand this is wise and on the other hand it reduces our ability to advance the quality of life for people and may hinder the advancement of our civilization. But in closing it is important to realize the importance of personal development in the form of becoming wise men and women. Wise people transcend conventional thinking that is corrupt in nature like materialism, elitism and manipulation of the masses.

'CHAPTER 20'

'The Global Religion Paradigm'

If we want to examine paradigms in our country and the world we can not disclude the religion paradigm. The religion paradigm has been with human beings from the beginning of recorded history. We had the ancient Mayens who worshiped Gods and even offered up human sacrifices (141). We had ancient Egypt with all of their Gods, for example the Egyptian sun god RA (142). We had ancient Israel with the single God who named himself "I Am" (143). We had the roman Gods, (144) the Gods of Ancient Greece (145) and the Norse Gods like Odin and Thor (146). We had Christianity with Jesus being God and at one with God the Father and God the Holy Spirit. This is the Christian trinity (147). We have Islam with the words of God coming from the Prophet (148). We have the Hindu religion with its many Gods and ancient texts (149).

Religion has shaped human systems of spirituality and moral codes for thousands of years. Even now, our paper currency in the United States reads "In God we Trust". Our founding fathers were Christians for the most part. Many people, in spite of our freedom of religion, consider the United States a so called Christian country. Yet Christianity does not run our country. We have a President not a Pope. In spite of this fact, sessions of Congress begin with a Prayer from the Congressional Chaplin (150).

So what about Atheists (151)? Can we call Atheism a religion? We can, but they will not appreciate it in the slightest bit. I can however in my view call Atheism a belief system or philosophy. An Atheist chooses to believe in nothing. The interesting thing about Atheist is the fact that they believe we are the most advanced animal on the planet. Yet they accept the moral code and laws of our religious founding fathers. Killing is wrong, stealing is wrong, and so forth. Why would the most advanced predator on the planet accept such moral nonsense? The answer to that question is the existence of the religious paradigm and it's code of morality and laws that they live under. If we are animals, then killing and every other false notion of evil should be considered morally correct. Yet we see that most atheists follow the rules of the law and basic morality, or common decency. I'm not saying this to pick on all of the Atheist. I say it to demonstrate the power and influence of the religious paradigm.

Yet in some cases we have people who operate outside of all morality. In my experience people like psychopaths love nothing more than to chain someone to a pillar in the basement and then do what they do. Some criminals in my opinion were simply unfortunately influenced by either bad people or poor parenting. Psychopaths are born, Sociopaths are made (usually by some form of abuse) (152). This is a substantial difference. An intelligent psychopath will more often than not kill people. Yet with sociopaths we see on television and in the movies that most serial killers are sociopaths. Some are and some are not. You may even know a sociopath and not even realize it. Just look for a lack of genuine emotion and a total lack of empathy. They are often narcissistic but they are not all killers. Some of them are just fine being antisocial and hanging around the house all day. Psychopaths are often charismatic and charming.

It would however seem that these people for the most part operate outside of the religious paradigm.

What other people generally operate outside of the religious paradigm? If we look back at the Directional Paradigm of Technology we find plenty of people who do. The smartest people in the technology paradigm are scientists and math wizards known as a theoretical physicists. These are people like Einstein and many we have never heard of. These are the people who discovered evolution and the big bang (theory). A theory is not a fact. In short it is a highly educated guess that is usually written in the form of a math problem. This math language takes up five chalkboards using symbols that only their community of wizards understand. Many great advances have come from this math language used by truly gifted people. Einstein is world renowned for his theory of relativity (153) which has actually been partially proven to be true. So it is no longer a theory. We know that timespace exist and that space and light bends. This opens endless other possibilities in the advancement of science.

In this technological community of math brain wired people we have certain codes of conduct that exist if you want to be part of the club in opinion. For one thing you must not be some religious moron who thinks that some God or other intelligence created the universe. Because technology is the end all of reality for these people in the scientific community. Can we say science is their religion? On at least some level I would say this is a philosophy. So with this big bang theory (154) we are taught that thirteen billion years ago a massive explosion took place and the universe was born into existence. The origin of this explosion is a mystery. Some scientists believe that we have billions of parallel universes spanning multiple dimensions and there was no beginning at all (155). Any way you want to view this is fine. But I personally have my own theory. Nothing from your computer to your shoes to the universe can simply create itself. I realize that the brilliant people we are talking about would dismiss this as idiotic nonsense from some idiot. If you believe in self creation I respect your opinion and I'm not here to preach. It is however important to note that the Directional Paradigm of Technology does shape at least some people's belief system. It is viewed as the educated and intelligent way to view reality and truth.

With regard to wisdom, must we assume that these genius level math wizards possess immense wisdom? Not remotely, for example Einstein in spite of his IQ treated his wife with utter neglect and cheated on her (156). She was not really a priority in my opinion. It is said that Einstein would be so deep in thought that he would accidentally walk into walls. Is this a wise man, or is this a guy who was so eccentric that he did not even possess common sense? Would you want Einstein watching your back in a fox hole? With all due respect I can say I admire his brilliance but his behavior? Not so much. Religion however has begun to work it's way into science at least a little bit. Terms like intelligent design (157) are being embraced by some in this elite club. Some would even be willing to look at the possibility that some advanced alien race may have created everything including us (158). With the new discovery of so many distant alien planets being viewed by the most modern telescopes, alien life is almost assumed (159). But in the end it is up to you the reader to search for truth in this world brimming with options.

So in spite of the fact that we have Atheist who have the right to be Atheist. Is religion a good thing? Sometimes it is and sometimes it is not. For example, if some guy walks up to me at the gas station with a pamphlet about Jesus and asks me, are you saved? Well, honestly I would, like many of you find this annoying. I would say something like I'm all set, thanks. If he pushes it I will lets just say 'dismiss' him. But the real question becomes, is he hurting anyone or is he out committing crimes? No he isn't, he is doing what 'fundamentalist Christians' do, he's out witnessing to people to bring them to God's salvation. This is what his church teaches him to do. In the world of the protestant Christianity we have around twenty thousand or more denominations at this point (160). They range from liberal to highly extreme. An extreme example would be some evangelical churches mainly in Appalachia that practice the handling of rattle snakes and even drink venom in their Christian Church (162). Probably not a safe place for kids in Sunday School. In essence if a religion has a code of morality and they are not hurting anyone they are at a minimum adding to basic morality in society. So even if you don't agree with any given religion, if they are producing a sense of morality and decency in their congregation, it's a good thing for society.

As far as I know we don't still have people worshiping Roman, Greek or norse Gods. I have never heard of anyone worshiping Egytian Gods in today's world. People practicing the Hindu religion seem to be able to integrate into our society. Jewish people have lived with us for hundreds of years and do no harm at all. All of this is positive for a safe society. It's the very simple concept that religion is the opposite of chaos if the religion is good in its teachings. Islam kind of depends on where you are. In my opinion if I walk down Main Street Tehran Iran with a crucifix hanging out of my shirt. I might just get hanged in the public square from some small crane in front of a cheering crowd the next morning at dawn. Or maybe not, they might just imprison me as an infidel spy. Yet many Islamic people are trying to embrace more liberal views in their religion (163). Many Islamist in the United States get along with just fine and open businesses.

This gradual change we see in Islam makes some Islamist absolutely furious in my view. They hate to see what they view as true Islam being desecrated by thier own people not practicing strict Sharia Law. We call these people Radical Islamic Extremist (164). These extremists view themselves as the faithful. It is not Islamophobic to recognise the fact that Islam is not just a religion, it is a system of government. So this makes Islam a very complicated religion to understand. We all for the most part, I believe, know that Saudi Arabia beheads its own citizens along with many other atrocities. Yet the world for many years has been all too eager to buy oil from them. This may upset people in the western world. But it also upsets the Radical Islamic Extremist. They find it sacrilegious that they do business with the infidels sub humans. Osama Bin Laden was one of these people from Saudi Arabia. In observing all of this within the world of Islam makes me consider the possibility that Terrorism is the result of Islamic Liberalism. As we see in the many uprisings in Iran and other countries like Egypt, the younger people are unhappy. In essence, the more people in the Islamic faith that become liberal. The more we will see extremist in Islam trying anything they can to stop it in my opinion. As we prepare our military to leave Afghanistan in my view. The Taliban is salivating to take over the government in place and create a strict Islamic State.

These religious attempts at revolting against the Ayatollah in Iran simply brings down the hammer on the common people (165). Yet over time the younger people will become the leaders. What do these young people and even some older people want? They want what we live in free countries. Things like the internet and TV and Facebook and ultimately, they want freedom of religion. We can only hope they succeed, but this also presents dangers. There is no telling how far a radical Islamic government will go to stop this from happening. In recent news reports, riots have erupted in Iran. At the time I'm writing this, the Iranian government has already killed a thousand people (165). I would not be at all surprised if our intelligence agencies are doing everything they can to encourage liberal Islam. This is not fact, this is just a guess on my part. This sort of influential role on the part of our government in altering regimes is however a fact. The intelligence community is highly skilled in affecting any population they desire. They use everything from social media to people on the ground to attempt to start a revolution. This takes time but eventually they will get it done.

The biggest positive I see in religion on a global scale is the fact these religions and philosophies inspire wisdom. Buddhism is not a religion, it is a philosophy. The idea is self enlightenment, or you could call it self development. The goal is to grow in wisdom. We also see this in the Catholic and other Christian churches. People are told they should become the person God wants them to be. This requires a lifetime of spiritual development and growth through prayer and community. The same principles apply to Judaism. Jewish people grow over the course of an entire lifetime and practice what Christians would call the Old Testament Law of Moses. Regardless of what you believe as a free person if you wish to improve yourself and gain wisdom, you can. One important thing in every religion, philosophy, atheism or other belief system, is who you trust.

Just because a person is in a leadership position does not automatically make them a wise or even a good person. If your going to allow yourself to be influenced by anyone, they need to be vetted by you. You never want to just go along with the religious crowd, or any other crowd for that matter. Trust and respect are developed over time and by a person's own observation of a so called leader. You would do this with any stranger you meet if your wise. Preachers and Philosophers are not an exception to this rule. Only the best should do. Your worth it, especially if your children are involved. In closing this chapter I would advise anyone in any system to avoid fanaticism. It's not even remotely healthy, it only separates you from everyone else and creates more fanaticism. All cults have this fanaticism in common.

CHAPTER 21

'The States'

Some people have asked the question, why do we even need States? Other countries do not have them so why do we? The States are an important check and balance on the Federal Government (166). States can make their own laws and they have their own elected officials on both the State and Town levels. If we only existed as one nation without States we would have the Federal Government as the Supreme Authority. States have the right to differ in certain laws and federal laws apply to all States. For example we do not have Federal Laws on all firearms sales. Each State can apply their own gun laws. However we do have a list of Federal gun laws (167). These laws include a requirement for the sales of weapons by a gun store owner to possess a Federal Firearms License. Another law is the prohibition of sales to the general public of what is labeled as a class two firearm. This includes sound suppressors or 'silencers' and fully automatic machine guns. You can't just go out and buy a mini gun at the gun store that fires over two thousand rounds per minute.

In the past we have seen a ban on so called assault rifles, this law expired and was not reenacted. So in the present you can buy an assault weapon. Depending on which State you live in you may only be able to buy a smaller magazine or clip as they are incorrectly called. In Chicago you have a gun free zone established by the State of Missouri. Abortion rights are a federal law (168) and at this time we have States passing their own laws on abortion. These cases will end up in the Supreme court. Guns and abortions are just two issues within the States. Other laws like States Taxes and Toll Roads are other examples varying from State to State. In my opinion this division of our country into States in very important to our Freedom.

If we only had the Federal Government in charge we would only have Federal Laws. If we only had Federal Laws we would only have Federal Law Enforcement. So imagine for a moment that the entire country was Policed by one law enforcement agency. As it stands now we have Town and State Police agencies. These agencies must stay within their respective jurisdictions. In my experience, in extreme cases Local Police police agencies can call for mutual aid from other towns and the State Police. Once the major incident is over every agency returns to its proper jurisdiction. A massive Federal Law Enforcement agency would number at around 800,000 officers. This is in effect an army in its size. We have seen some local Police Departments investigated for corruption by State Police or the FBI. What would happen if the Federal Police became corrupt? Would they be investigated by the Military? Do we want our Military to Police Law Enforcement? No we do not. The Military must stay out of domestic law enforcement.

In spite of this, if massive rioting takes place a State Governor may call in the National Guard to establish order. I personally disagree with this practice. I believe that the military should be held in reserve for war alone. If we get invaded then the Military should be on our streets. In the case of rioting I think it would be better if we had interstate mutual aid conducted by law enforcement. A system could be established in which a State could restore order by bringing in outside law enforcement agencies to get this done. So the States are very important in protecting our freedoms from any possibility of the Federal Government becoming too powerful.

With my idea of Non Adversarial Systems website you would be participating in all three areas. Federal State and local politics. So as an example you would open the website and by default you would have access to the Federal Government and your perspective State and Town governments in separate tabs of the pages. This would be established by your voter ID number and the other security measures in entering the website. You can answer polls and vote in all three areas right online as we discussed earlier. The system won't allow a person from Indiana to vote on local issues in Texas. If you move you will need to establish your new address and State for you to gain access to the system. If you have homes in multiple States you must designate a home address and home State that you are only allowed to participate in through the website. Some of you may be reading this and saying, this sounds like a full time job. You may be saying who has time to keep track of Federal State and Local governance? The answer to this is the idea of taking our time on all of this governance. You will have a month to vote for these things as we discussed earlier. We don't need to rush anything. Having a month will get things done much faster then our current congress.

However, it is possible for a National Emergency to require immediate action by the Government. In a case like an attack from another country that requires immediate action the Executive Council would have to act immediately, especially if it is a nuclear attack. If the Council needs a Declaration of War in a matter of hours they would have the right to convien congress for a quick emergency vote if it is needed. Yet we the people could also have a quick vote in an emergency that allows for say three days. In that case you would get an emergency alert via text that there is an emergency vote. Most wars won't require a vote in an hour. Yet if God forbid Russia launches a nuclear attack against us, our leaders must be able to react immediately on our behalf. It may be very unlikely but all scenarios must be covered in a system of Government. As far as the existence of States go, we definitely need them.

CHAPTER 22

'What does the Future Hold'

Given the name of this chapter, you may be wondering if I fancy myself some sort of prophet or Nostradamus figure. Not at all, I make no claims of knowing the future. However I can explore possible outcomes given the paradigms described in this book. So the question is what can the future hold? For starters, we can start with our Adversarial system of Government. We know that over the vast course of time that both the Democratic and Repoublican parties will gain power. A close family relative has described this changing of the guard as a great pendulum that swings back and forth and ends up in the center left or center right. I highly respect his opinion as he has confidence that it will all work itself out in time. Many people have faith in the current system.

As for me I don't share his optimism about the future. I will however say that it is possible that things will work out in the end. From another perspective if center right and center left is the existing paradigm it will be born out this way in Non Adversarial System as well. As I said, I'm not a prophet. In my view I see the system of government devolving into system so divided that it may collapse in certain scenarios. I am writing this in December of 2019. The President Donald Trump is undergoing an impeachment process by the House of Representatives. It is highly believed that this impeachment will pass in the house. Then it moves to the Senate where it is very likely to fail in actually convicting the President. So with this, many in the world of our so called politics view this impeachment as something that will help Trump. He may just be getting a boost to his base and be elected to a second term as President. I would tend to agree with this notion, history demonstrated this with the 'half impeachment' of Bill Clinton that

helped him in getting reelected. This sort of impeachment only solidifies the base of the 'victim' of the senseless politically motivated impeachment. However it is possible that Trump will lose however unlikely it seems at the moment.

The Democratic Party is changing at a very rapid pace in this moment in my opinion. It would appear that the embrace of Socialism on the far left side of the Democratic Party is taking over the party. Nancy Pelosi is the Speaker of the House seems to be having trouble controlling her party as its leader. We have seen four women called 'the squad' (169) emerge as a far left power base. Every Democrat in Congress seems afraid of them for some mysterious reason. People in the Democratic party are often more centrist and far less socialistic than the so called 'squad'(169). Yet they do not attack them at all. As a result of this we see candidates for President like Elizabeth Warren adopt all of their extremist ideas from Socialism to Medicare for all. This new (quite limited) idea of a green new deal will cost more money than we have. Regardless of the outcome of the coming Presidential election, at some point this new Democratic Party will come into power. I can say with confidence based on history that the pendulum will swing left again for the Democrats sooner or later.

So why is this a problem? The millennial generation is highly supportive of this notion of Socialism in our Government. They want free healthcare and education and to be saved from climate change Armageddon scenarios they believe in. For these millennials this an emergency and they are being highly noticed by the Democrats. The squad (169) and the self admitted socialist Bernie Sanders are in essence the voice of the millenials. This millennial movement even if Trump is reelected will continue to grow and more and more. Democrats will jump on this bandwagon to get elected. So if this comes to fruition as the current trend supports, we will inevitably embrace a new paradigm of Socialism as our form of government. As we previously discussed in the financial paradigm chapter, this will be a disastrous paradigm shift.

The eventual outcome of socialism is a failed State in bankruptcy lacking opportunity for business success. The financial American Dream will no longer be possible. This is the very reason that we need an option three in the form of a Fair Compensation Act as we discussed. So again I could be wrong about this but the evidence does lean this way in my opinion with regards to the economy and emergence of millennial Socialism as a new direction.

So that covers the potential dangers of economic ruin via a new Socialist America. Many people say this will never happen. Yet Bernie Sanders is a legend to the younger people. What does this say? That is the question moving forward as these millennials get older and come into power. Is this a type of emergency that we should consider with the fate of our country? I believe it must be prevented openly by the people and our so called leaders. Do we need a new system? To explore this questions information, we need to take another look at these millennials. What do really want? Why do they see a need to have a new system of government? What is motivating all of this. The millennials see the government as a corrupt system that fails to provide for the people. They feel that our political leaders only care about themselves or the rich members of our society.

Given what we discussed in the chapter about today's visionaries it becomes obvious that the only options they have to choose from are Globalism and Socialism. In this book a third option is offered in the form of a Non Adversarial System of Government. We can eliminate Socialism as an option. I believe that people will embrace this idea. They will be awake to the fact that they are not going to tolerate being lied to and manipulated by our leaders and the media. The millenials are rebellious against our current system. What sounds more appealing to the people, ending lies in politics and empowering the people? Or Socialism that leads to economic collapse while we are still being deceived by Socialist leaders? If we give the people a system with both a Non Adversarial System of Government and a Fair Compensation Act, it will be very appealing. A true government of the people without lies and manipulation. This idea of a Federal website for all as we discussed is actually very possible upon further review. Every time I watch TV I am hearing about this revolutionary 5G broadband system coming online (170). This is a massive increase of internet power that will lead to many innovations. Therefore an Online Government System of the people having the power, is quite possible.

So in essence this entire book is designed to reveal the hidden paradigms that we never questioned. The reason this matters at all is because we are at an inflection point of change in our country. The new choices in this inflection are simply inferior and unintelligent in my opinion. So I believe it's time to find option three and that is what I'm trying to lay out here. If the people want this it will happen. If they want Socialism it will eventually happen. If we don't offer better options to the people they will make choices based on what they are currently offered and that is a fact. So constitutional scholars who feel that we have the best system ever will likely call my ideas nonsense. They may say that the framers had it right. I agree that they had it right in the 1700's. I'm not saying that the constitution needs to be eliminated at all.

Yet given what we explored in the directional paradigm of technology they would have never even imagined this time we live in. In fact, if the founding fathers were here right now they would probably change everything in light of the present paradigms. They would throw every lobbyist in jail and put limits on the media in all likelihood just for starters. So we don't need a new constitution but I would say that we certainly do need an upgrade of the system to match our new world. We also need this system to encourage people to develop mentally. Why does this matter? It's simple, technology has advanced 20 times further than human thinking has advanced. In other words, our thought processes need to catch up to a world so technologically advanced that we have nuclear weapons.

As it stands now the battle cry of the young and ultra liberals is Socialism. The solution they seek is now the problem we desperately need to prevent. I can imagine a battle cry of the people saying, "no more lies, no more rhetoric, give the power to the people, give us fair compensation and businesses a fair system of law. "You work for us", "we will not be deceived anymore". "We are taking back our country". "You will listen to the will of the people."

Am I some sort of insurrectionist rebel? No not at all, I don't ever condone a violent uprising. Am I trying to manipulate you? No, I'm trying to un-manipulate you. Am I trying to deceive you? No, I'm attempting to show you that you are being deceived. Do I want to start some sort of grass roots movement? No I've spent enough time leading and I'm not interested in doing it.. Am I trying to start a revolution, not even a little bit. That would be absurd and crushed in two days. Do I want to run for political office. Not in this lifetime. Do I believe that our current paradigms are manufactured by some secret society in some grand conspiracy? No, I believe that we naturally evolved to this point because of the paradigms never questioned. In other words, this is what our Founding Fathers ideas have mutated into over hundreds of years.

These ideas would need to be examined by the individual and either accepted or rejected on their own merits. Everything I am talking about is based on free people being free people. The impact of such a new system in my opinion would make us an even more powerful nation. The people and businesses would become richer. We may in fact become mega-power. This as I mentioned earlier is an attempt at achieving a win win scenario on many of the levels we have discussed. But in the end I believe it is time to become a truly advanced civilization that transcends lies, manipulation and rhetoric. A country that pays people what they actually deserve. Other nations would be sure to follow. We would in essence prevent any sort of coming calamity as we saw in the moral decay and inward collapse of the Roman Empire. The end goals are simple, no Adversarial System and all it's deception, and a fair system of compensation that includes the preservation of free market capitalism. Laws against criminal organizations, and different kinds of Education. I think it is time for a change. I will ask the question once more, "If not now, then when?"

REFERENCES

(1)Robinson, Melia. "25 Photos Show What Iran Looked like before the 1979 Revolution Turned the Nation into an Islamic Republic." *Business Insider*, Business Insider, 11 Feb. 2019, https://www.businessinsider.com/iran-before-the-revolution-in-photos-2015-4

(2)"Iranian Revolution." *Wikipedia*, Wikimedia Foundation, 14 Dec. 2019, https://en.wikipedia.org/wiki/Iranian_Revolution.

(3)-, TUW Media, et al. "TUW Media." *The United West*, 12 Apr. 2018, https://www.theunited-west.org/2018/04/12/dearborn-michigan-americas-biggest-muslim-no-go-zone-what-could-2018-elections-bring.

(4)"Application of Sharia Law by Country." *Wikipedia*, Wikimedia Foundation, 16 July 2016,https://en.wikipedia.org/wiki/Application_of_sharia_law_by_country.

(5)History.com Editors. "ISIS." *History.com*, A&E Television Networks, 10 July 2017, https://www.history.com/topics/21st-century/isis.

(6)"Christian Schism." *Wikipedia*, Wikimedia Foundation, 21 Feb. 2019, https://en.wikipedia.org/wiki/Christian_schism.

(7)"Esoteric Interpretation of the Quran." *Wikipedia*, Wikimedia Foundation, 4 Dec. 2019, https://en.m.wikipedia.org/wiki/Esoteric_interpretation_of_the_Quran.

(8)U.S. Census Bureau. "Behind the 2018 U.S. Midterm Election Turnout." *The United States Census Bureau*, 16 July 2019, https://www.census.gov/library/stories/2019/04/behind-2018-united-states-midterm-election-turnout.html.

(9)"Lobbying in the United States." *Wikipedia*, Wikimedia Foundation, 4 Dec. 2019, https://en.wikipedia.org/wiki/Lobbying_in_the_United_States.

(10)"What Happened To British Loyalists After The Revolutionary War?" *NPR*, NPR, 3 July 2015, https://www.npr.org/2015/07/03/419824333/what-happened-to-british-loyalists-after-the-revolutionary-war.

(11)"The United States Constitution - The U.S. Constitution Online." *The United States Constitution - The U.S. Constitution Online - USConstitution.net*, https://usconstitution.net/const.html.

(12)"Salaries of Members of the United States Congress." *Wikipedia*, Wikimedia Foundation, 26 Nov. 2019, https://en.wikipedia.org/wiki/Salaries_of_members_of_the_United_States_Congress.

(13)"Democratic Republic." *Wikipedia*, Wikimedia Foundation, 10 Dec. 2019, https://en.wikipedia.org/wiki/Democratic_republic

(14) "Moral Relativism." *Wikipedia*, Wikimedia Foundation, 30 Nov. 2019, https://en.wikipedia.org/wiki/Moral_relativism.

(15) Lam, Kristin. "Chicago Experiences Most Violent Weekend of 2019: 52 Shot, 10 Killed." *USA Today*, Gannett Satellite Information Network, 4 June 2019, https://www.usatoday.com/story/news/nation/2019/06/03/chicago-52-shot-10-killed-most-violent-weekend-2019/1334351001/.

(16) Crime In The 1940's VS Now? *Extrano's Alley*, https://extranosalley.com/crime-in-the-1940s-vs-now/.

(17) "Adversarial Process." *Wikipedia*, Wikimedia Foundation, 25 Jan. 2019, https://en.wikipedia.org/wiki/Adversarial_process.

(18)"Jonestown." *Wikipedia*, Wikimedia Foundation, 20 Nov. 2019, https://en.wikipedia.org/wiki/Jonestown.

(19)"Carvana: Buy & Finance Used Cars Online: Skip The Dealership." *Carvana.com*, https://www.carvana.com/?utm_source=google&utm_medium=sem_b&utm_campaign=1880664463&utm_content=70171589676&utm_target=kwd-4186217408&utm_creative=386493140526&utm_device=c&utm_adposition=1t1&utm_rw=1&gclid=EAIaIQobChMIxLfzvuq25gIVRTOMCh2IGQY3EAAYASAAEgL32fD_BwE.

(20) "Narcissist." *Merriam-Webster*, Merriam-Webster, https://www.merriam-webster.com/dictionary/narcissist.

(21)"Due Process." *Wikipedia*, Wikimedia Foundation, 7 Dec. 2019, https://en.wikipedia.org/wiki/Due_process.

(22) "Public Defender." *Wikipedia*, Wikimedia Foundation, 9 Nov. 2019, https://en.wikipedia.org/wiki/Public_defender.

(23)https://en.wikipedia.org/wiki/Dream_Team_(law)

(24)"Efren Saldivar." *Wikipedia*, Wikimedia Foundation, 4 Nov. 2019, https://en.wikipedia.org/wiki/Efren_Saldivar.

(25) Hager, Eli. "A Major Player in Law Enforcement Says It Will Stop Using a Method That's Been Linked to False Confessions." *Business In-*

sider, Business Insider, 10 Mar. 2017, https://www.businessinsider-.com/reid-technique-false-confessions-law-enforcement-2017-3.

(26)"Bench Trial." *Wikipedia*, Wikimedia Foundation, 24 Nov. 2019, https://en.wikipedia.org/wiki/Bench_trial.

(27) "Supreme Court of the United States." *Wikipedia*, Wikimedia Foundation, 8 Dec. 2019, https://en.wikipedia.org/wiki/Supreme_Court_of_the_United_States.

(28) Collins, Matthew, and Matthew Collins. "[What's the Difference?]: AR-15 vs M4." *Pew Pew Tactical*, 2 May 2019, https://www.pewpewtactical.com/ar15-vs-m4-difference/.

(29) "Virginia Tech Shooting." *Wikipedia*, Wikimedia Foundation, 12 Dec. 2019, https://en.wikipedia.org/wiki/Virginia_Tech_shooting.

(30) Handelman, Stephen, and Justice News. "Black Market Accounts for Two of Three Federal Weapons Prosecutions: Report." *The Crime Report*, 12 June 2019, https://the-crimereport.org/2019/06/11/black-market-accounts-for-two-out-of-three-federal-weapons-prosecutions-report/.

(31) Reporter, HealthDay staff HealthDay. "Ruth Bader Ginsburg Released From Hospital After Health Scare." *WebMD*, WebMD, 25 Nov. 2019, https://www.webmd.com/healthy-aging/news/20191125/ruth-bader-ginsburg-released-from-hospital-after-health-scare#1.

(32) Robbins, James S. "Progressive Democrats Let Their 'Policy Freak Flags' Fly, Want to Take ocialist-radical-initiatives-congress-column/2573566002/.

(33)"Political Correctness." *Wikipedia*, Wikimedia Foundation, 12 Dec. 2019, https://en.wikipedia.org/wiki/Political_correctness.

(34)Classicalycourt. "Here's How Many Days Congress Will Spend Away from the Office in 2018." *CNBC*, CNBC, 29

Mar. 2018, https://www.cnbc.com/2018/03/29/heres-how-many-days-congress-will-spend-away-from-the-office-in-2018.html.

(35) "Congressional Pension." *Wikipedia*, Wikimedia Foundation, 10 Nov. 2019, https://en.wikipedia.org/wiki/Congressional_pension.

(36) "Rhetoric: Definition of Rhetoric by Lexico." *Lexico Dictionaries | English*, Lexico Dictionaries, https://www.lexico.com/en/definition/rhetoric.

(37) "Veto." *Merriam-Webster*, Merriam-Webster, https://www.merriam-webster.com/dictionary/veto.

(38) "Commander-in-Chief." *Wikipedia*, Wikimedia Foundation, 7 Dec. 2019, https://en.wikipedia.org/wiki/Commander-in-chief.

(39)"United States Electoral College." *Wikipedia*, Wikimedia Foundation, 13 Dec. 2019, https://en.wikipedia.org/wiki/United_States_Electoral_College.

(40) "Keep the Electoral College." *Cato Institute*, 15 Dec. 2012, https://www.cato.org/publications/commentary/keep-electoral-college.

(41) "Twelfth Amendment to the United States Constitution." *Wikipedia*, Wikimedia Foundation, 8 Dec. 2019, https://en.m.wikipedia.org/wiki/Twelfth_Amendment_to_the_United_States_Constitution.

(42) "Campaign Finance in the United States." *Wikipedia*, Wikimedia Foundation, 15 Dec. 2019, https://en.wikipedia.org/wiki/Campaign_finance_in_the_United_States.

(43) "Green New Deal." *Wikipedia*, Wikimedia Foundation, 1 Dec. 2019, https://en.wikipedia.org/wiki/Green_New_Deal.

(44) Vaida, Bara. "Medicare for All: FAQ." *WebMD*, WebMD, 20 Nov.

2019, https://www.webmd.com/health-insurance/news/20191120/medicare-for-all-faq.

(45) "Political Polarization." *Pew Research Center*, Pew Research Center, 12 June 2014, https://www.pewresearch.org/topics/political-polarization/.

(46) "2000 United States Presidential Election." *Wikipedia*, Wikimedia Foundation, 15 Dec. 2019, https://en.wikipedia.org/wiki/2000_United_States_presidential_election.

(47) Ney, P G, and A R Wickett. "Mental Health and Abortion: Review and Analysis." *Psychiatric Journal of the University of Ottawa : Revue De Psychiatrie De L'Universite D'Ottawa*, U.S. National Library of Medicine, Nov. 1989, https://www.ncbi.nlm.nih.gov/pubmed/2682716.

(48) "Unborn Victims of Violence Act." *Wikipedia*, Wikimedia Foundation, 3 Nov. 2019, https://en.wikipedia.org/wiki/Unborn_Victims_of_Violence_Act.

(49) "United States Population (LIVE)." *Worldometers*, https://www.worldometers.info/world-population/us-population/.

(50) Kenton, Will. "Affordable Care Act (ACA)." *Investopedia*, Investopedia, 18 Nov. 2019, https://www.investopedia.com/terms/a/affordable-care-act.asp.

(51)Inskeep, Steve, and Ashley Westerman. "Why Is China Placing A Global Bet On Coal?" NPR, NPR, 29 Apr. 2019, https://www.npr.org/2019/04/29/716347646/why-is-china-placing-a-global-bet-on-coal.m-Webster, Merriam-Webster, https://www.merriam-Party to Far Left." USA Today, Gannett Satellite Information Network, 15 Jan. 2019, https://www.usatoday.com/story/opinion/2019/01/15/progressive-democrats-propose-hard-left-s

(52) "Bernie Sanders: Scientists Say We Have 'Eight or Nine Years' Before Cities Are Underwater Due to Climate Change." *Climate Depot*, 22 Nov. 2019, https://www.climate-depot.com/2019/11/22/bernie-sanders-scientists-say-we-have-eight-or-nine-years-before-cities-are-underwater-due-to-climate-change/.

(53) "Volcanic Winter." *Wikipedia*, Wikimedia Foundation, 6 Dec. 2019, https://en.wikipedia.org/wiki/Volcanic_winter.

(54) "Socialist State." *Wikipedia*, Wikimedia Foundation, 15 Dec. 2019, https://en.wikipedia.org/wiki/Socialist_state.

(55) "Anti-Austerity Movement in Greece." *Wikipedia*, Wikimedia Foundation, 14 Dec. 2019, https://en.wikipedia.org/wiki/Anti-austerity_movement_in_Greece.

(56) "Globalism." *Wikipedia*, Wikimedia Foundation, 15 Dec. 2019, https://en.wikipedia.org/wiki/Globalism.

(57) "New World Order (Politics)." *Wikipedia*, Wikimedia Foundation, 21 Nov. 2019, https://en.wikipedia.org/wiki/New_world_order_(politics).

(58) Liphshiz, Cnaan, and Jta. "George Soros Praises Elizabeth Warren, Says Globalism Will Defeat Trump's Nationalism." *Haaretz.com*, 27 Oct. 2019, https://www.haaretz.com/us-news/soros-praises-elizabeth-warren-says-globalism-will-defeat-trump-s-nationalism-1.8030901.

(59) "George Soros." *Wikipedia*, Wikimedia Foundation, 13 Dec. 2019, https://en.wikipedia.org/wiki/George_Soros#Conspiracy_theories_and_threats.

(60) "John Lennon – Imagine." *Genius*, 11 Oct. 1971, https://genius.com/John-lennon-imagine-lyrics.

(61) "Victory in Europe Day." *Wikipedia*, Wikimedia Foundation, 11 Dec. 2019, https://en.wikipedia.org/wiki/Victory_in_Europe_Day.

(62) "Derivatives Market." *Wikipedia*, Wikimedia Foundation, 14 Oct. 2019, https://en.wikipedia.org/wiki/Derivatives_market.

(63) Davis, Marc. "U.S. Government Financial Bailouts." *Investopedia*, Investopedia, 18 Nov. 2019, https://www.investopedia.com/articles/economics/08/government-financial-bailout.asp.

(64) Scheiber, Noam. "Obama To Bankers: Beware The Pitchforks." *The New Republic*, 3 Apr. 2009, https://newrepublic.com/article/48854/obama-bankers-beware-the-pitchforks.

(65) Borunda, Daniel. "Mexico Drug Cartel Violence Flares as Mexicles, Gente Nueva War Rattles Valley of Juárez." *El Paso Times*, El Paso Times, 19 June 2019, https://www.elpasotimes.com/story/news/local/juarez/2019/06/19/mexico-violence-mexicles-gente-nueva-gang-war-rattles-valley-juarez/1489874001/.

(66) Sherman, Erik. "One in Five U.S. Companies Say China Has Stolen Their Intellectual Property." *Fortune*, Fortune, 1 Mar. 2019, https://fortune.com/2019/03/01/china-ip-theft/.

(67) *Bloomberg.com*, Bloomberg, https://www.bloomberg.com/graphics/2018-china-superpower/.

(68) Hinsbergh, Gavin Van. "China's Top 10 Largest Cities, the Most Populous in China." *China Highlights*, 10 Nov. 2019, https://www.chinahighlights.com/travelguide/top-large-cities.htm.

(69) "Xinjiang Re-Education Camps." *Wikipedia*, Wikimedia Foundation, 14 Dec. 2019, https://en.wikipedia.org/wiki/Xinjiang_re-education_camps.

(70) Overthecap.com. "Quarterback Contracts and Salaries." *Over the Cap*, https://overthecap.com/position/quarterback/.

(71) "Income Inequality in the United States." *Wikipedia*, Wikimedia Foundation, 12 Dec. 2019, https://en.wikipedia.org/wiki/Income_inequality_in_the_United_States.

(72) "Colin Kaepernick." *Wikipedia*, Wikimedia Foundation, 11 Dec. 2019, https://en.wikipedia.org/wiki/Colin_Kaepernick.

(73) *Bloomberg.com*, Bloomberg, https://www.bloomberg.com/news/articles/2018-08-02/apple-becomes-first-u-s-company-to-hit-1-trillion-market-value.

(74) DeCambre, Mark. "Bill Gates Says He's Happy to Pay $20 Billion in Taxes, but Warren's Plan Will Make Him 'Do a Little Math on What I Have Left over'." *MarketWatch*, 24 Nov. 2019, https://www.marketwatch.com/story/bill-gates-im-happy-to-pay-20-billion-in-taxes-but-warrens-plan-will-make-me-do-a-little-math-on-what-i-have-left-over-2019-11-07.

(75) Probasco, Jim. "9 States With No Income Tax." *Investopedia*, Investopedia, 21 Nov. 2019, https://www.investopedia.com/financial-edge/0210/7-states-with-no-income-tax.aspx.

(76) "Bernie Sanders Demonstrates How $15 Minimum Wage Constricts Hours Worked." *CNSNews.com*, https://www.cnsnews.com/commentary/hans-bader/bernie-sanders-demonstrates-how-15-minimum-wage-constricts-hours-worked.

(77) "Bernanke Doctrine." *Wikipedia*, Wikimedia Foundation, 6 May 2015, https://en.wikipedia.org/wiki/Bernanke_doctrine.

(78) "Russian Interference in the 2016 United States Elections." *Wiki-*

pedia, Wikimedia Foundation, 5 Dec. 2019, https://en.wikipedia.org/wiki/Russian_interference_in_the_2016_United_States_elections.

(79) "2019 China Military Strength." *Global Firepower - World Military Strength*, https://www.globalfirepower.com/country-military-strength-detail.asp?country_id=china.

(80) "2019 United States Military Strength." *Global Firepower - World Military Strength*, https://www.globalfirepower.com/country-military-strength-detail.asp?country_id=united-states-of-america.

(81) "Putin, before Vote, Says He'd Reverse Soviet Collapse If He Could: Agencies." *Reuters*, Thomson Reuters, 2 Mar. 2018, https://www.reuters.com/article/us-russia-election-putin/putin-before-vote-says-hed-reverse-soviet-collapse-if-he-could-agencies-idUSKCN1GE2TF.

(82) "United States Forces Korea." *Wikipedia*, Wikimedia Foundation, 20 Nov. 2019, https://en.wikipedia.org/wiki/United_States_Forces_Korea.

(83) Blakemore, Erin. "The Korean War Hasn't Officially Ended. One Reason: POWs." *History.com*, A&E Television Networks, 28 Feb. 2019, https://www.history.com/news/korean-war-peace-treaty-pows.

(84) "List of North Korean Missile Tests." *Wikipedia*, Wikimedia Foundation, 13 Dec. 2019, https://en.wikipedia.org/wiki/List_of_North_Korean_missile_tests.

(85) Weller, Chris. "This Satellite Photo Shows Just How Blacked-out North Korea Is at Night." *Business Insider*, Business Insider, 15 Oct. 2015, https://www.businessinsider.com/north-korea-is-pitch-black-at-night-2015-10.

(86) Kuhn, Anthony. "Why South Korea Is Sending $8 Million In Food Aid To North Korea." *NPR*, NPR, 9 June 2019, https://www.npr.org/sec-

tions/goatsandsoda/2019/06/09/730441007/why-aid-wont-fix-north-koreas-recurring-food-shortages.

(87) Harden, Blaine. "How North Korea Feeds Its Impoverished People a Steady Diet of Anti-U.S. Paranoia." *History.com*, A&E Television Networks, 18 Apr. 2018, https://www.history.com/news/north-korea-u-s-nuclear-war-threat.

(88) Rosenberg, Joel C. "Islamic Extremists Are Trying to Hasten the Coming of the Mahdi." *National Review*, National Review, 11 Sept. 2015, https://www.nationalreview.com/2015/09/radical-islam-iran-isis-apocalytpic-messiah-mahdi/.

(89) Seligman, Lara. "Top U.S. General: It's 'Very Possible' Iran Will Attack Again." *Foreign Policy*, 23 Nov. 2019, https://foreignpolicy.com/2019/11/23/very-possible-iran-will-attack-again-top-us-general-says/.

(90) McGreal, Chris, and Ewen MacAskill. "Israel Should Be Wiped off Map, Says Iran's President." *The Guardian*, Guardian News and Media, 26 Oct. 2005, https://www.theguardian.com/world/2005/oct/27/israel.iran.

(91) "Israel–United States Relations." *Wikipedia*, Wikimedia Foundation, 25 Nov. 2019, https://en.wikipedia.org/wiki/Israel–United_States_relations.

(92) "Iran–Russia Relations." *Wikipedia*, Wikimedia Foundation, 24 Nov. 2019, https://en.wikipedia.org/wiki/Iran–Russia_relations.

(93) "The Late, Great Planet Earth." *Wikipedia*, Wikimedia Foundation, 15 Dec. 2019, https://en.wikipedia.org/wiki/The_Late,_Great_Planet_Earth.

(94) amanda_m_macias. "US Military Releases New Im-

ages of Japanese Oil Tanker Attack." *CNBC*, CNBC, 20 June 2019, https://www.cnbc.com/2019/06/17/us-military-releases-new-images-of-japanese-oil-tanker-attack.html.

(95) "United States Withdrawal from the Joint Comprehensive Plan of Action." *Wikipedia*, Wikimedia Foundation, 13 Nov. 2019, https://en.wikipedia.org/wiki/United_States_withdrawal_from_the_Joint_Comprehensive_Plan_of_Action.

(96) Horsley, Scott. "Saudi Attack Draws New U.S. Sanctions Against Iran." *NPR*, NPR, 20 Sept. 2019, https://www.npr.org/2019/09/20/762762360/saudi-attack-draws-new-u-s-sanctions-against-iran.

(97) "MIM-104 Patriot." *Wikipedia*, Wikimedia Foundation, 22 Oct. 2019, https://en.wikipedia.org/wiki/MIM-104_Patriot.

(98) "Iran Nuclear Sites May Be beyond Reach of 'Bunker Busters.'" *Reuters*, Thomson Reuters, 12 Jan. 2012, https://www.reuters.com/article/us-iran-nuclear-strike/iran-nuclear-sites-may-be-beyond-reach-of-bunker-busters-idUSTRE80B0WM20120112.

(99) "Islamophobia." *Wikipedia*, Wikimedia Foundation, 5 Dec. 2019, https://en.wikipedia.org/wiki/Islamophobia.

(100) "Xenophobia." *Wikipedia*, Wikimedia Foundation, 16 Dec. 2019, https://en.wikipedia.org/wiki/Xenophobia.

(101) "2019 Iranian Protests." *Wikipedia*, Wikimedia Foundation, 15 Dec. 2019, https://en.wikipedia.org/wiki/2019_Iranian_protests.

(102) "Volunteer Military." *Wikipedia*, Wikimedia Foundation, 1 Sept. 2019, https://en.wikipedia.org/wiki/Volunteer_military.

(103) "CBU-97 Sensor Fuzed Weapon." *Wikipedia*, Wikimedia Foundation, 7 Dec. 2019, https://en.wikipedia.org/wiki/CBU-97_Sensor_Fuzed_Weapon.

(104) "M1 Abrams." *Wikipedia*, Wikimedia Foundation, 14 Dec. 2019, https://en.wikipedia.org/wiki/M1_Abrams.

(105) "Lockheed Martin F-22 Raptor." *Wikipedia*, Wikimedia Foundation, 11 Dec. 2019, https://en.wikipedia.org/wiki/Lockheed_Martin_F--22_Raptor.

(106) "M1 Garand." *Wikipedia*, Wikimedia Foundation, 12 Dec. 2019, https://en.wikipedia.org/wiki/M1_Garand.

(107) "A-10 Thunderbolt II." *Military.com*, https://www.military.com/equipment/a-10-thunderbolt-ii.

(108) "United States Intelligence Community." *Wikipedia*, Wikimedia Foundation, 30 Nov. 2019, https://en.wikipedia.org/wiki/United_States_Intelligence_Community.

(109) "Edward Snowden." *Wikipedia*, Wikimedia Foundation, 9 Dec. 2019, https://en.wikipedia.org/wiki/Edward_Snowden.

(110) Turner, Bill. "The Biggest Leaks Revealed by Edward Snowden." *Prefuse*, 18 Aug. 2019, https://prefuse.org/edward-snowden-leaks.

(111) "Patriot Act." *Wikipedia*, Wikimedia Foundation, 25 Nov. 2019, https://en.wikipedia.org/wiki/Patriot_Act.

(112) "Guantanamo Bay Detention Camp." *Wikipedia*, Wikimedia Foundation, 10 Dec. 2019, https://en.wikipedia.org/wiki/Guantanamo_Bay_detention_camp.

(113) "September 11 Attacks." *Wikipedia*, Wikimedia Foundation, 29 Nov. 2019, https://en.wikipedia.org/wiki/September_11_attacks.

(114) Crowley, Michael. "Nuclear Terrorism Keeps Obama Up at Night, and It Should." *Time*, Time, 26 Mar. 2014, https://time.com/39131/barack-obama-nuke-manhattan-new-york/.

(115) "Boston Marathon Bombing." *Wikipedia*, Wikimedia Foundation, 14 Dec. 2019, https://en.wikipedia.org/wiki/Boston_Marathon_bombing.

(116) "Abu Bakr Al-Baghdadi." *Wikipedia*, Wikimedia Foundation, 1 Dec. 2019, https://en.wikipedia.org/wiki/Abu_Bakr_al-Baghdadi.

(117) Engel, Richard, and Daniel Arkin. "Kurdish Informant Provided Key Intel in Operation That Killed ISIS Leader Abu Bakr Al-Baghdadi." *NBCNews.com*, NBCUniversal News Group, 29 Oct. 2019, https://www.nbcnews.com/news/world/kurdish-source-provided-key-intel-operation-killed-isis-leader-abu-n1072921.

(118) "Millennials." *Wikipedia*, Wikimedia Foundation, 16 Dec. 2019, https://en.wikipedia.org/wiki/Millennials.

(119) Nbc. "3 Arrested After Videos of NYPD Cops Doused With Buckets of Water Go Viral." *NBC New York*, NBC New York, 25 July 2019, https://www.nbcnewyork.com/news/local/arrest-water-bucket-nypd-police-monahan-gang-member/1522784/.

(120) Allyn, Bobby. "Ex-Dallas Officer Who Killed Man In His Own Apartment Is Found Guilty Of Murder." *NPR*, NPR, 1 Oct. 2019, https://www.npr.org/2019/10/01/765788338/ex-dallas-officer-who-killed-neighbor-in-upstairs-apartment-found-guilty-of-murd.

(121) "How the Fight or Flight Response Works." *The American Institute of Stress*, 21 Aug. 2019, https://www.stress.org/how-the-fight-or-flight-response-works.

(122) "Cops (TV Program)." *Wikipedia*, Wikimedia Foundation, 8 Dec. 2019, https://en.wikipedia.org/wiki/Cops_(TV_program).

(123) "Miranda Warning." *Wikipedia*, Wikimedia Foundation, 1 Oct. 2019, https://en.wikipedia.org/wiki/Miranda_warning.

(124) "Industrial Revolution." *Wikipedia*, Wikimedia Foundation, 9 Dec. 2019, https://en.wikipedia.org/wiki/Industrial_Revolution.

(125) "Geometric Progression." *Wikipedia*, Wikimedia Foundation, 19 Nov. 2019, https://en.wikipedia.org/wiki/Geometric_progression.

(126) Strickland, Jonathan, and Patrick J. Kiger. "How Area 51 Works." *HowStuffWorks Science*, HowStuffWorks, 20 Sept. 2019, https://science.howstuffworks.com/space/aliens-ufos/area-517.htm.

(127) "Thomas Savery." *Wikipedia*, Wikimedia Foundation, 17 Nov. 2019, https://en.wikipedia.org/wiki/Thomas_Savery.

(128) Frohlich, Thomas C. "Sheltering the Homeless: These 48 Major US Cities Face Growing Homeless Populations." *USA Today*, Gannett Satellite Information Network, 7 Oct. 2019, https://www.usatoday.com/story/money/2019/10/07/48-major-us-cities-struggling-to-shelter-growing-homeless-population/40242171/.

(129) Public Affairs. "What Is the U.S. Opioid Epidemic?" *HHS.gov*, Https://Plus.google.com/ HHS, https://www.hhs.gov/opioids/about-the-epidemic/index.html.

(130) "Naloxone." *Wikipedia*, Wikimedia Foundation, 16 Dec. 2019, https://en.wikipedia.org/wiki/Naloxone.

(131) Midgette, Gregory, and Beau Kilmer. "Americans' Spending on Illicit Drugs Nears $150 Billion Annually; Appears to Rival What Is Spent on Alcohol." *RAND Corporation*, 20 Aug. 2019, https://www.rand.org/news/press/2019/08/20.html.

(132) "Drugs, Inc." *Wikipedia*, Wikimedia Foundation, 7 Aug. 2019, https://en.wikipedia.org/wiki/Drugs,_Inc.

(133) "Opioid Crisis Has Frightening Parallels to Drug Epidemic of Late

1800s." *LiveScience*, Purch, https://www.livescience.com/60559-opi-oid-crisis-echoes-epidemic-of-1800s.html.

(134) Narea, Nicole. "Trump Wants to Call Mexican Drug Cartels 'Terrorist Organizations.'" *Vox*, Vox, 12 Dec. 2019, https://www.vox.com/policy-and-politics/2019/12/12/20999191/trump-mexican-drug-cartels-terrorist-organizations-mexico-sinaloa-transnational-criminal-trafficking.

(134) "Crusades." *Wikipedia*, Wikimedia Foundation, 16 Dec. 2019, https://en.wikipedia.org/wiki/Crusades.

(135) History.com Editors. "Adolf Hitler." *History.com*, A&E Television Networks, 29 Oct. 2009, https://www.history.com/topics/world-war-ii/adolf-hitler-1.

(136) "Lawrence Taylor." *Wikipedia*, Wikimedia Foundation, 6 Dec. 2019, https://en.wikipedia.org/wiki/Lawrence_Taylor.

(137) Gringlas, Sam. "Activists Disrupt Harvard-Yale Rivalry Game To Protest Climate Change." *NPR*, NPR, 24 Nov. 2019, https://www.npr.org/2019/11/24/782427425/activists-disrupt-harvard-yale-rivalry-game-to-protest-climate-change.

(138) AbigailJHess. "Bill Gates: US College Dropout Rates Are 'Tragic'." *CNBC*, CNBC, 10 Oct. 2017, https://www.cnbc.com/2017/10/10/bill-gates-us-college-dropout-rates-are-tragic.html.

(139) "Elitism." *Wikipedia*, Wikimedia Foundation, 11 Dec. 2019, https://en.wikipedia.org/wiki/Elitism.

(140) "Overview of Learning Styles." *Overview of Learning Styles*, https://www.learning-styles-online.com/overview/.

(141)"Human Sacrifice in Maya Culture." *Wikipedia*, Wikimedia Foundation, 16 Dec. 2019, https://en.wikipedia.org/wiki/Human_sacrifice_in_Maya_culture.

(142) "List of Egyptian Deities." *Wikipedia*, Wikimedia Foundation, 17 Dec. 2019, https://en.wikipedia.org/wiki/List_of_Egyptian_deities.

(143) "I Am That I Am." *Wikipedia*, Wikimedia Foundation, 10 Dec. 2019, https://en.wikipedia.org/wiki/I_Am_that_I_Am.

(144) "List of Roman Deities." *Wikipedia*, Wikimedia Foundation, 2 Dec. 2019, https://en.wikipedia.org/wiki/List_of_Roman_deities.

(145) "List of Greek Mythological Figures." *Wikipedia*, Wikimedia Foundation, 11 Nov. 2019, https://en.wikipedia.org/wiki/List_of_Greek_mythological_figures.

(146) "Norse Mythology." *Wikipedia*, Wikimedia Foundation, 11 Dec. 2019, https://en.wikipedia.org/wiki/Norse_mythology.

(147) "Trinity." *Wikipedia*, Wikimedia Foundation, 8 Dec. 2019, https://en.wikipedia.org/wiki/Trinity.

(148) "Islam." *Wikipedia*, Wikimedia Foundation, 15 Dec. 2019, https://en.wikipedia.org/wiki/Islam.

(149) "Hinduism." *Wikipedia*, Wikimedia Foundation, 15 Dec. 2019, https://en.wikipedia.org/wiki/Hinduism.

(150) "Chaplain of the United States House of Representatives." *Wikipedia*, Wikimedia Foundation, 29 Oct. 2019, https://en.wikipedia.org/wiki/Chaplain_of_the_United_States_House_of_Representatives.

(151) "What Is Atheism?" *American Atheists*, https://www.atheists.org/activism/resources/about-atheism/.

(152) Duignan, Brian. "What's the Difference Between a Psychopath and a Sociopath? And How Do Both Differ from Narcissists?" *Encyclopædia Britannica*, Encyclopædia Britannica, Inc., https://www.bri-

tannica.com/story/whats-the-difference-between-a-psychopath-and-a-sociopath-and-how-do-both-differ-from-narcissists.

(153) "Theory of Relativity." *Wikipedia*, Wikimedia Foundation, 11 Dec. 2019, https://en.wikipedia.org/wiki/Theory_of_relativity.

(154) "The Big Bang Theory." *Wikipedia*, Wikimedia Foundation, 10 Dec. 2019, https://en.wikipedia.org/wiki/The_Big_Bang_Theory.

(155) ChoMay, Adrian, et al. "Stephen Hawking's (Almost) Last Paper: Putting an End to the Beginning of the Universe." *Science*, 3 May 2018, https://www.sciencemag.org/news/2018/05/stephen-hawking-s-almost-last-paper-putting-end-beginning-universe.

(156) Staff, Bio. "Albert Einstein: God-like in Science, Human in Love." *Biography.com*, A&E Networks Television, 14 June 2019, https://www.biography.com/news/einstein-love-life-wives-affairs-letters.

(157) https://en.wikipedia.org/wiki/Intelligent_design

(158) Martin, Sean. "Big Bang Theory Wrong? 'Aliens Created Universe and Control Everything around Us'." *Express.co.uk*, Express.co.uk, 6 Sept. 2019, https://www.express.co.uk/news/science/1174825/big-bang-theory-aliens-black-hole-alien-universe-space-discovery-columbia-university.

(159) "7 Earth-Sized Planets Found Orbiting Star 39 Light-Years Away | CBC News." *CBCnews*, CBC/Radio Canada, 11 July 2017, https://www.cbc.ca/news/technology/7-earth-like-planets-discovered-1.3992156.

(160) "Just How Many Protestant Denominations Are There?" *National Catholic Register*, http://www.ncregister.com/blog/sbeale/just-how-many-protestant-denominations-are-there.

(162) "Snake Handling in Religion." *Wikipedia*, Wikimedia Foundation,

12 Dec. 2019, https://en.wikipedia.org/wiki/Snake_handling_in_religion.

(163) "Liberalism and Progressivism within Islam." *Wikipedia*, Wikimedia Foundation, 17 Dec. 2019, https://en.wikipedia.org/wiki/Liberalism_and_progressivism_within_Islam.

(164) "Islamic Extremism." *Wikipedia*, Wikimedia Foundation, 11 Dec. 2019, https://en.wikipedia.org/wiki/Islamic_extremism.

(165) "2019 Iranian Protests." *Wikipedia*, Wikimedia Foundation, 18 Dec. 2019, https://en.wikipedia.org/wiki/2019_Iranian_protests.

(166) History.com Editors. "Constitution." *History.com*, A&E Television Networks, 27 Oct. 2009, https://www.history.com/topics/united-states-constitution/constitution.

(167) "Gun Law in the United States." *Wikipedia*, Wikimedia Foundation, 13 Dec. 2019, https://en.wikipedia.org/wiki/Gun_law_in_the_United_States.

(168) https://en.wikipedia.org/wiki/Roe_v._Wade

(169) "The Squad (United States Congress)." *Wikipedia*, Wikimedia Foundation, 16 Dec. 2019, https://en.wikipedia.org/wiki/The_Squad_(United_States_Congress).

(170) https://en.wikipedia.org/wiki/5G